Phil Lee

111 Places
in Nottingham
That You
Shouldn't Miss

Photographs by Rachel Ghent

T0348701

emons:

Bibliographical information of the Deutsche Nationalbibliothek
The Deutsche Nationalbibliothek lists this publication in
the Deutsche Nationalbibliografie; detailed bibliographical data
are available on the internet at http://dnb.d-nb.de.

© Emons Verlag GmbH
All rights reserved
© Photographs by Rachel Ghent, except see p. 238
© Cover Icon: shutterstock.com/untitled
Layout: Eva Kraskes, based on a design
by Lübbeke | Naumann | Thoben
Maps: altancicek.design, www.altancicek.de
Basic cartographical information from Openstreetmap,
© OpenStreetMap-Mitwirkende, OdbL
Editing: Martin Sketchley
Printing and binding: Grafisches Centrum Cuno, Calbe
Printed in Germany 2024
ISBN 978-3-7408-2261-3
First edition 2023
Revised second edition, June 2024

Guidebooks for Locals & Experienced Travellers
Join us in uncovering new places around the world at
www.111places.com

Foreword

I was born and raised in Nottingham, which must be a good start for somebody writing *111 Places in Nottingham That You Shouldn't Miss*. And in many ways it was indeed fortuitous, though I was not prepared for the many surprises that were in store for me during my research.

I knew, for instance, of the splendid Bennerley Viaduct, but I was not aware of the efforts made to preserve it by a group of volunteers. And I was also aware that Thomas Cranmer, the martyred Archbishop of Canterbury, came from Nottinghamshire, but I didn't know that the spot where he came to listen to the church bells had survived. I had also heard of Watson Fothergill, the inventive Victorian architect who specialised in the Gothic Revival style, but I hadn't fully appreciated just how talented he was. I knew of the imposing Newton Building, but I had no idea that it was planned as part of a much larger project. I had heard of the alabaster carvings in Strelley Church, but never realized just how beautiful they were. And then there were the historical niceties I stumbled across, like the spot where two Luddites fired a pistol at a leading hosier; the lace factory where the heir to the business joined the British army and was killed in Dublin while suppressing the Easter Rising; the local duke who prosecuted three Bottesford women for being witches; and the 'murder stone' commemorating the untimely death of Bessie Sheppard.

I always thought I knew my city well, but during my explorations, I realised just how much more there was to Nottingham than I had realised. So, while I was delighted to write this book, I am even more excited to share these places and stories with everyone who is interested in discovering all that the city has to offer.

Whether you are a local or a visitor, photographer Rachel Ghent and I both hope you will find delight in many of the places on the following pages.

111 Places

1 28–30 Pelham Street

Where J. M. Barrie learnt his craft

James Matthew Barrie (1860–1937), Scottish creator of *Peter Pan*, came to Nottingham by happenstance in 1883. The story goes that his sister spotted an advertisement for a lead writer at the *Nottingham Journal*, and encouraged her brother to apply. He submitted some of his university essays in his application and, rather to his surprise, was given the job without delay.

At the time, the *Journal* was Nottingham's pre-eminent newspaper, and it was here that Barrie soon won the respect of his colleagues with his well-crafted, often laconic articles written under the name of a Greek mythological figure, Hippomenes. In 1888, Barrie's ruminations on his journalistic life in Nottingham were distilled into *When a Man's Single*. The city may also have provided some inspiration for his later children's writings, as certain parts of Peter Pan's character may well have been inspired by the antics of a local street urchin the author had observed, and certain features of *Neverland* seem to have been inspired by the Arboretum (see ch. 8). That said, other aspects of Barrie's life, principally the death of his older brother, and his friendship with the Llewelyn Davies boys, were much more influential.

In 1884, the *Nottingham Journal* dispensed with Barrie's services and the author left the city, never to live here again. The paper itself didn't last much longer – it was incorporated into the *Nottingham Daily Express* in 1887, though the name was later resurrected before finally disappearing in 1953. Nonetheless, the building the *Nottingham Journal* movedinto on Pelham Street in 1860 – and where Barrie worked – has survived. Tanners estate agent occupies the premises today and, although the ground floor has been clumsily modernised, the double bank of brightly painted, neo-Gothic windows above are a flash of Victorian style. There's a unassuming plaque celebrating the Barrie connection on the building too.

Address 28–30 Pelham Street, Nottingham, NG1 3EG | Getting there Local bus (most lines) or tram to the city centre | Hours The interior of the building has been turned into an estate agents, but the façade is always visible | Tip In the 1920s, Graham Greene followed in Barrie's footsteps by working at the *Nottingham Journal*; his office was elsewhere in the city, a five-minute walk away at 19–20 Upper Parliament Street (see ch. 33).

2 32 Victoria Crescent
Where David met Frieda

In 1912, a smartly dressed young man strolled up to the door of a handsome suburban house on Victoria Crescent in Nottingham. That man was David Herbert Lawrence (1885–1930) and the house was owned by his favourite professor, Ernest Weekley, who had invited him for lunch. In the event, the invitation was a professorial mistake: Ernest wasn't in, but his wife, Frieda, was. Frieda took an immediate shine to the young visitor – so much so that she and Lawrence eloped together later that year, leaving the professor high and dry.

Predictably, this created something of a scandal in polite society, not least because Frieda had three young children. Nonetheless, the pair stayed together until Lawrence's death from tuberculosis. The furore that arose from their elopement was the first of the many travails that punctuated Lawrence's life, prompting him to travel far and wide – his 'savage pilgrimage' as he once called it.

Lawrence was born in the coal-mining town of Eastwood, just outside Nottingham, but he despised his father, a colliery worker, and adored his mother – a family dynamic that inspired much of his early work, whose earthy realism stirred much condemnation. Today, Lawrence is best known for his novels *Sons and Lovers*, *The Rainbow* and *Women in Love*, but towards the end of his life it was *Lady Chatterley's Lover* that dominated the headlines. First published in 1928, this story of a relationship between a working-class man and an upper-class woman included much swearing and enough explicit sex to ensure that it didn't appear in unexpurgated form until 1960 – and only then after a famous obscenity trial.

Back in Eastwood, Lawrence's literary exploits may have cut little ice, but his right-wing politics did: the town was then a Labour-voting heartland, and immediately after the author died no-one in his home town even thought of erecting a monument in his honour.

Address 32 Victoria Crescent, Mapperley, Nottingham, NG5 4DA | **Getting there** Bus 45 to Private Road, then a five-minute walk; please note that if driving, Victoria Crescent is only accessible from the Mansfield Road end of Private Road – the other end has an automatic barrier through which only residents' vehicles can pass. | **Hours** Private residence, always visible from the outside during daylight hours, but please be mindful of residents' privacy. | **Tip** From Victoria Crescent, it's a 10-minute walk to Bronte, a first-rate Turkish café at 589 Mansfield Road.

3 __ 33 Castle Gate
Be thankful, my dear child, for all you have

It's a crying shame that 33 Castle Gate, a stone's throw from the inner ring road (Maid Marian Way), has been left to wrack and ruin. A Grade II listed building, the tidy symmetries of this three-storey town house date back to the middle of the 18th century, though the building was re-fronted and stuccoed a century later, and white-washed thereafter.

The original interior is long gone – and there's currently no access – but hopefully someone, somewhere will see its value, especially as this was once the home of the poet, hymn-writer, author and anti-slavery campaigner Ann Gilbert (1782–1866). Born Ann Taylor in London, Gilbert married a Congregationalist minister in her early 30s and moved to Nottingham a few years later. Over the next decades, Ann became a leading local light in all things radical, founding, for example, the Nottingham Ladies Society for the Relief of Negro Slaves and a refuge for 'unfortunate women', all whilst conducting a voluminous correspondence with her friends and relatives, and even writing a lengthy autobiography.

Perhaps unfairly, however, it's for her observations on Nottingham's Reform riots of 1831 that she is mostly remembered. From the rooftop of her home here on Castle Gate, Gilbert had a bird's eye view of the burning of the castle in which 'Lights gleamed from window after window, and presently, tongues of fire leaped out amidst shouts and yells, piercing the air, as the flames did the darkness. Then followed crash after crash, molten lead began to pour from the roof, and the odour of burning cedar-wood penetrated everywhere'. Gilbert did not exactly approve of the riot, but she did sympathise with the reasons for it: the owner of the castle, the Duke of Newcastle, had helped stymy a Parliamentary Reform Bill, which would have greatly extended the vote – and this had infuriated many here in Nottingham.

Address 33 Castle Gate, Nottingham, NG1 7AR | Getting there Local bus (most lines) or tram to the city centre, then a five-minute walk | Hours Visible from the outside only | Tip The Nottingham Women's History Group (www.nottinghamwomenshistory.org.uk) has done an excellent job bringing women like Ann Gilbert to the fore.

4 Adams Building
Victorian extravaganza built for lace

Not a market at all, but rather the most historic part of Nottingham, the Lace Market was the centre of the world's lace industry during the second half of the 19th century. At its peak, in the 1890s, the industry employed 25,000, mostly female, workers here in the city – a prodigiously large work force by almost any standard. Nottingham lace was machine-made with a multitude of purposes – from curtains to tablecloths and clothing – but changing fashions meant that the industry started to decline in the 1920s, and by the 1970s it had almost completely withered away, leaving the imposing buildings of the Lace Market as witness to past glories.

The mightiest of these Victorian structures were the warehouses, which the factory owners used for storing, displaying and selling their products. The proudest of them all is the superb Adams Building, whose façade, with its handsome curved wings, is of fetching Italianate design, featuring alternating Ancaster stone and reddish brick. It was built in the 1850s at the behest of Thomas Adams (1807–1873), a sharp-elbowed lace manufacturer, who was candidly honest about his abilities, confessing that 'I can make money but I cannot make a speech'.

Money magnet he may have been, but Adams gave generously – and secretly – to a variety of local causes, and was, in true paternalistic fashion, concerned about the spiritual welfare of his work force: 'We desire to regard you as our fellow Christians,' he wrote to all 600 of them before moving into the Adams Building. True to his word, he built a basement chapel 'so that we may seek the blessing of God upon our daily labours'. It would be easy to be cynical about such noblesse oblige, but Adams took care of the physical as well as the spiritual, adding heating, washing facilities and a canteen to his premises. As a mark of the man, over 10,000 people attended his funeral.

Address Stoney Street, Nottingham, NG1 1NG | **Getting there** Local bus (most lines) or tram to the city centre, then a five-minute walk | **Hours** Not open to the public | **Tip** The Adams Building is now part of Nottingham College, so public access is restricted, but if you stroll round the back to St Mary's Gate, you can view the building's handsome rear façade and its capacious interior courtyard.

5 Alabasters of Strelley

Exquisite alabaster carvings in a fine old church

On the northwest edge of Nottingham, just beyond a sprawling council estate, Strelley is an odd little village, old and unruffled, its string of red-brick cottages trailing up to All Saints church, a delightful medieval structure perched on a grassy knoll. The church's mottled appearance comes from its seemingly haphazard mix of brick, stone and mortar, but the whitewashed interior is calmer, the short and wide nave leading to an intricately carved oak rood screen dating from the 1490s – though the rood itself was added in the 1920s. Beyond, in the chancel, are two magnificent alabaster altar tombs, the carving of which is simply breathtaking.

The first, in the centre, dates from around 1405, and depicts Sir Sampson and Elizabeth de Strelley; the knight, with his splendid moustache, is in his armour, whilst his wife wears a flowing gown with a fancy and fashionable 'Phoenician' headdress. Sampson's neck rests on the head of a strangled Saracen, whose tongue lolls out, and dogs rest at their feet, but in a show of tenderness, the couple are holding hands as they await the Resurrection.

Across the chancel, in a recess, the altar tomb of John and Sanchia de Strelley dates to around 1500. There's no hand-holding here, but rather the hands of each are clasped in prayer. There are more carved dogs – one worries at the bottom of Sanchia's dress – another strangled Saracen head (it was the de Strelley crest), and an amiable-looking lion lies at John's feet. John is also encased in his best suit of armour, but not his helmet, which allows his hair to flow down to his shoulders, whilst up above the couple is a veritable embankment of stone carving with saints, angels and coats of arms. Neither should you miss the choir stalls, or rather one of the misericords, depicting a Green Woman with limbs resembling branches and legs akimbo, as in a Sheela na gig, a female grotesque thought to have been used to ward off evil spirits.

Address Main Street, Strelley, Nottingham, NG8 6PE, www.allsaintschurchstrelley.org.uk |
Getting there Bus 77 to the Rose Inn, then a 20-minute walk; by car, it's a 20-minute drive
from central Nottingham | Hours Third Sun of the month noon–3pm; additional times
possible by prior arrangement with rosemarylwalker@icloud.com or collect the church
key from Strelley Hall reception next door (+44 (0)115 906 1200) | Tip All Saints church
is next to Strelley Hall, a large complex comprising the original hall and an assortment
of former agricultural buildings; the old stables have been turned into a pleasant café, the
Mulberry Tree (www.mulberrytreestrelley.co.uk); you can also wander round some parts of
the extensive grounds.

6 Alan Sillitoe's Birthplace

'What I'm out for is a good time' – Arthur Seaton

If there's one book that encapsulates post-war industrial Nottingham, it's Alan Sillitoe's *Saturday Night and Sunday Morning*. First published in 1958, this is the story of Arthur Seaton, a turbulent and rebellious working-class lad, who operates a factory lathe during the day and drinks hard and long in the pub at night. Seaton's irreverent humour, complicated sex life and anarchic behaviour – never mind his class – managed to get the book classified as a product of one of the 'Angry Young Men', a group of authors that included the likes of John Osborne and Kingsley Amis, although this categorisation didn't please Sillitoe at all.

Sillitoe's childhood in Nottingham was far from idyllic. Born in 1928, his family was poor, and his father allegedly violent. Sillitoe left school at the age of 14 to work at Nottingham's Raleigh bicycle factory. Later, he joined the Royal Air Force, before spending several years abroad and ultimately settling in and around London. Since his death in 2010, there have been sporadic efforts to have a statue erected in his honour, but these have proven unsuccessful so far. The most specific reminder of Sillitoe's connection to his home city is the plaque attached to the house of his birth at 38 Manton Crescent, out near Nottingham University.

All that said, it is perhaps the 1960 film of the book that hits more of the right notes, with a magnificent performance by Albert Finney as Arthur Seaton – all to a script by Sillitoe himself. Parts of the film were shot in Nottingham, and although most of the locations are long gone, the White Horse, at 313 Ilkeston Road, Lenton, has just about managed to hang on. It's no longer a pub, but its attractive green and cream exterior tiling has survived, albeit now marooned amongst the University tower blocks that have replaced the terrace houses and factories of yesteryear, the past somewhat vaguely recalled by 'Sillitoe Court' on 'Sillitoe Way'.

Address 38 Manton Crescent, Lenton Abbey, Nottingham, NG9 2GE | **Getting there** Local bus 36 to Manton Crescent | **Hours** Private residence, viewable from the outside during daylight hours, but please be considerate of residents' privacy. | **Tip** The White Horse was one of the film locations used for *Saturday Night and Sunday Morning*; to get there, take bus 28 or 30 from outside the Victoria Centre in the city centre to Middleton Street, and then it's a two-minute walk.

7 The Angel Microbrewery

Real ale at one of the best pubs in Nottingham

At the heart of the Lace Market, The Angel Microbrewery – formerly the Old Angel – is one of the best pubs in the city centre, attracting a varied clientele from students bent on a big night out, through to real ale aficionados content to sip and savour. There's been a pub on this corner since at least the 1800s, but it has had a complicated history, and the present pub occupies two adjoining premises – hence the two entrances: the one on the left, with its fancy columns, leads into a series of small and cosy snugs, whilst the entrance on the right gives access to a longer bar, decked out in informal boho style, with bare-brick walls and pot-pourri furnishings.

Live acts perform on the floor above this longer bar in what was originally a Nonconformist chapel – an unusual arrangement with, presumably, saints up above and sinners down below; you can spot the chapel windows from outside. Nowadays, The Angel is a gastro pub offering a tasty and filling menu that features such traditional delights as fish and chips, through to more unusual options such as the Korean fried burgers. There's also a wide range of beers on tap, including the products of the on-site microbrewery: try, for example, their tangy Pale Angel.

During its long history, The Angel has had more than its fair share of drama, not least events inextricably linked to the excessive consumption of alcohol: in 1831, the soused owner – a certain Robert Pearson – died when he rolled down the stairs, and 30 years later Edward Hulse, a young lace worker, simply dropped out of a third-storey window. There are less blood curdling connections too – the author Alan Sillitoe (see ch. 6) drank here, and mentions the pub in his novel *The Open Door*. And in the 1980s and 1990s, the chapel was a grungy sort of place, which attracted a number of famous bands in their early days, most memorably Oasis in 1994.

Address 7 Stoney Street, Nottingham, NG1 1LG, +44 (0)7908 942417, www.theangelmicrobrewery.co.uk | Getting there Local bus (most lines) or tram to the city centre, then a five-minute walk | Hours Mon–Wed noon–midnight, Thu–Sat noon–1.30am, Sun noon–11pm | Tip The Angel showcases a first-rate programme of live music in its chapel; details are posted on the website.

8 The Arboretum

Nottingham's prettiest and most interesting park

Opened in May 1852, in front of a crowd of 30,000 delighted citizens, the Arboretum is Nottingham's oldest, most central and most beautiful park. The main entrance, with its weathered stone columns, is on Waverley Street, on its west side. From here, footpaths slope up into the park, whose grassy lawns are set amidst a canopy of mature trees, including beeches, Canadian maples, Turkish oaks, copper beeches, dawn redwoods and atlas cedars.

Near the entrance, you'll also spy an attractive little pond, whose murky waters accommodate an assortment of ducks, as well as a set of large, antique bird cages. These now house a modest collection of pretty little birds that have been donated to the park, but formerly one was the home of 'Cocky', a much-loved (and very noisy) sulphur-crested cockatoo. Cocky sadly died in 1968 at the age of 114 – doubly remarkable, considering the assorted tidbits local children tried to feed him.

Further into the park, set on top of a wide stone platform, is a war memorial celebrating Britain's imperial past. The four cannons here (including two replicas) were captured at Sevastopol during the Crimean War of the 1850s, whilst the Chinese Bell Tower immediately above them was looted from Canton during the Second Opium War (1856-1860): a local regiment was involved in the storming of that city during the war, which was, notionally at least, fought for the right of Europeans to export opium to the Chinese. Nearby, and perhaps rather more palatable today, is a statue honouring the Chartist Feargus O'Connor (1796–1855). A charismatic campaigner for land and electoral reform, O'Connor was a popular Nottingham MP in the 1840s, but later suffered a mental breakdown from which he never recovered. Visitors can exit the park on the east side via a stone tunnel that runs under Addison Street, before reaching the park's eastern gates on North Sherwood Street.

Address Waverley Street, Nottingham, NG7 4HF | **Getting there** Local bus (most lines) or tram to the city centre, then a five-minute walk | **Hours** Open daylight hours; free | **Tip** Wet your whistle at the park's tiny little café, The Arboretum, just beside the entrance gates on Waverley Street.

9 Attenborough Reserve

Best birdwatching site in the region

One of the region's most popular family attractions, Attenborough Nature Reserve occupies a substantial slab of lake, wetland, grassland and scrub at the confluence of the rivers Erewash and Trent, around seven miles south-west of Nottingham. It was opened in 1966 by none other than Sir David Attenborough, but is not named after him: it takes its name from the adjacent village of Attenborough.

Owned by the Nottinghamshire Wildlife Trust since 2020, the reserve mainly comprises former gravel pits, which were released to become wetlands once all the available gravel and sand had been extracted. Today, the reserve is best known for the variety of its bird life. Over 250 species have been spotted here with, for example, visitors standing a good chance of spotting resident kingfishers and overwintering bitterns or even, on occasion, the rare migratory purple heron. The reserve incorporates half a dozen mini-lakes – or 'ponds' – including the Main Pond, Beeston Pond and the Church Pond. Three clearly signed footpaths worm their way round these ponds, and there are several bird hides, some of which are elevated.

Of the three walks – none of which could be described as 'strenuous' – the longest is the Kingfisher Trail (3.7 miles), while the shortest is the Tufted Duck Trail (2 miles). Maps and wildlife information are prominently displayed at the main entrance, and it's here that a short footbridge spans marshy terrain to reach the centre of the reserve, its Nature Centre. This is housed in an attractive modern building with an asymmetrical gulls-wing roof of steel, supported by walls of timber and laminate panels. The shop sells a wide variety of nature-related items, ranging from hedgehog homes and nest boxes through to bird seed and feeders, while at the back there's a dedicated outdoor education area, primarily for visiting school groups.

Address Barton Lane, Chilwell, Nottinghamshire, NG9 6DY, +44 (0)115 972 1777, www.nottinghamshirewildlife.org | **Getting there** The Nature Reserve is a 25-minute drive from Nottingham, but it's better to take the train to Attenborough railway station, and then it's a 10-minute walk to the reserve via Church Lane | **Hours** Car park daily 8am–8pm; Nature Centre: winter daily 9am–4pm, Sat & Sun 9am–6pm; summer Mon–Fri 9am–5pm, Sat & Sun 9am–6pm | **Tip** From Attenborough Nature Reserve, a footpath loops its way along the River Trent to reach, after about two miles, the pleasant Canalside Heritage Centre (www.canalsideheritagecentre.org.uk), at the point where the Nottingham & Beeston canal meets the river.

10 Bendigo Thompson's Grave
Nottingham's answer to Muhammed Ali

In 1880, thousands lined the streets of Nottingham to watch the funeral cortège of the prize fighter Bendigo Thompson wind its way through the city – and The Times of London even published an obituary, a rare honour for a 'commoner'. A remarkable man, Bendigo – born William Abednego Thompson – was an imaginative self-publicist. This began with his name: he claimed to be one of a set of triplets named Shadrach, Meshach and Abednego, after a Bible story in the Book of Daniel, in which three young men survived being thrown into a fiery furnace; his contemporaries were very familiar with the tale, but it was almost certainly a falsehood.

It is true, however, that this working-class lad had a tough upbringing, spending time in the Nottingham Workhouse before taking up bare-knuckle boxing as a teenager. Exceptionally agile with a rock-hard punch, Bendigo worked his way up through the pugilist ranks to become the heavyweight boxing champion of England in 1839 – a title he held against all comers for over a decade. His bitter local rival was Ben Caunt, a giant of a man whom Bendigo teased mercilessly during their several bouts. It was this teasing, as well as the running commentary Bendigo kept up through his fights – in a manner akin to Muhammed Ali – that made him extraordinarily popular: he pulled faces at his opponents; laughed at their missed punches; performed gymnastics, somersaults and handstands during fights, and composed rhymes mocking his rivals.

After he retired, Bendigo hit the skids, becoming a desperate drunk. That might have been that, but for a chance visit to a Revivalist meeting, where he was converted to Christianity. Thereafter, he became a lay preacher, his sermons attracting large crowds. He was buried in St Mary's Cemetery, now St Mary's Rest Garden, and this is where you will find his stone tomb, guarded by a lion.

Address St Mary's Rest Garden, Bath Street, Nottingham, NG1 1DA | Getting there Local bus (most lines) or tram to the city centre, then a five-minute walk to the west entrance of St Mary's Rest Garden; follow the path and after a couple of minutes you'll spot his grave – standing on its own, on the right-hand side of the path. | Hours St Mary's Rest Garden is open during daylight hours; free | Tip St Mary's Rest Garden adjoins Victoria Park, on the far side of which, at the corner of Robin Hood Street and Roden Street, is an especially handsome example of Victorian industrial architecture, the Bancroft's Lace Factory of 1869.

11 Bennerley Viaduct

The longest wrought-iron viaduct in England

The Bennerley Viaduct is a supreme example of Victorian industrial architecture, its graceful trestle piers sweeping across the flood plain of the Erewash River around eight miles north-west of Nottingham. Completed in 1877, the viaduct was built for the Great Northern Railway (GNR), which was keen to cash in on the lucrative business of transporting coal from the nearby mines.

At the time, viaducts were normally built of brick, but here the ground was subject to subsidence, so the architect-engineers opted for a much lighter structure with wrought-iron lattice work on both the bridge and its supporting piers, whose foundations are themselves of blue engineering bricks capped with stone. The end result is 1,452 feet (443m) long, with a maximum height of 60 feet (18m) – no wonder it was soon nicknamed 'The Iron Giant'. The engineers responsible were led by Richard Johnson (1827–1924). Johnson was an archetypal railway man, and an employee of GNR for many years, peppering the Midlands with his bridges whilst pushing the company to switch from iron to steel rails.

In 1968, Bennerley Viaduct was closed to rail traffic and left to its own devices, gradually disintegrating as the years passed by. Fortunately, this sad state of affairs attracted the attention of a band of volunteers, who are now incorporated as the Friends of Bennerley Viaduct. Slowly but surely, the Friends have attracted enough funding to both repair the viaduct and provide access to the public. New polycarbonate decking means it's possible to walk from one end of the viaduct to the other. There's ramp access from the west and, at time of writing, a ramp for easy access from the east is under construction, funded by the Levelling Up Fund. The best viewing points are on the east side, and the viaduct links in with the 30-mile Erewash Valley Trail, a popular cycling and walking route.

Address Newton Lane car park, just off the A 6096, Awsworth, Nottinghamshire, NG16 2SD | **Getting there** To get to the ramped west end of the viaduct, take the train to Ilkeston and from the station it's a 25-minute walk through the town and along the Erewash Valley Trail; to get to the ramped east end of the viaduct, it's a 25-minute drive from Nottingham to the Newton Lane car park, from where it's a pleasant 15-minute walk along the tow path beside the (disused) Nottingham canal | **Hours** Open access | **Tip** For more information about the projected construction of a visitor centre, café and car park, check out the Friends of Bennerley Viaduct website: www.bennerleyviaduct.org.uk. The work is scheduled to be completed by the end of 2024.

12 Bessie Sheppard Memorial

A brutal Georgian murder

In July 1817, a young woman by the name of Elizabeth (Bessie) Sheppard was walking back from Mansfield to her home in the village of Papplewick, a seven-mile journey along a country road near Nottingham. Sadly, it was the last journey she ever made. As she left Harlow Wood, she disturbed a certain Charles Rotherham, a 33-year-old itinerant scissor grinder, who was sleeping under a hedge. Seemingly without more ado, Rotherham killed Bessie, stealing both her shoes and her distinctive yellow umbrella. Rotherham then left the scene of the crime and sold the shoes at a nearby inn, though he accidentally left the umbrella behind – clearly, he was no master criminal. In the meantime, the body was discovered along with the murder weapon: a bloodstained hedge stake.

The police soon tracked down Rotherham, who had managed to get as far as Leicestershire, and he promptly confessed to the crime. There seems to have been no specific motive, though there were unsubstantiated rumours that Rotherham had met Sheppard when she stayed in Mansfield the night before. It is true, however, that Rotherham was no stranger to violence: he had been in the army for 18 years, and may well have fought at Waterloo. Whatever the truth, Rotherham was found guilty and hanged on Nottingham's Gallows Hill (see ch. 38) later that month.

That wasn't quite the end of the story, however: locals were so horrified by the murder that they clubbed together to have a commemorative stone marker placed where Bessie died. Such 'murder stones', installed at the sites of well-known murders, were popular in the early 19th century. Bessie's stone, which has been restored with a slate plaque, is still there – though it can be difficult to locate, as it's partly hidden by the undergrowth on the east verge of the A60 near Newstead Abbey.

THIS STONE IS ERECTED
TO THE MEMORY OF
ELIZABETH SHEPPARD
OF PAPPLEWICK
WHO WAS MURDERED
WHEN PASSING THIS SPOT BY
CHARLES ROTHERHAM
JULY 7TH 1817
AGED 17 YEARS

Address To get to Bessie's memorial stone, head north from the entrance to Newstead Abbey for just over a mile, and it's on the verge on the right – just beyond a bus stop and immediately behind the warning sign indicating a sharp right turn (though you can only see the back of this sign going in this direction). | Getting there By car, via the A 60. There's no designated parking space near the memorial stone – just pull in and park where you can. | Hours Open access | Tip The inn where Charles Rotherham left Bessie's umbrella was rebuilt in the 1840s and survives today as the Hutt Inn(www.chefandbrewer.com), opposite the entrance to Newstead Abbey.

13 __ Bestwood Colliery

When coal was king

Nottinghamshire has produced coal since medieval times, if not before. At first, it was only profitable to mine surface coal, but technological improvements in the middle of the 19th century made mining deeper seams feasible. As a result, no fewer than 16 new Nottinghamshire collieries came on-stream in the 1870s, and production leapt from just over three million tons in 1854, to 12 million in 1880; by the end of the century, there were 23,000 Nottinghamshire miners – both men and boys.

Opened in 1871, one of these new pits was here at Bestwood, where the coal fired an adjacent ironworks. The principal beneficiaries were the Lancaster family, who leased the colliery, and the owner of the Bestwood Estate, William Beauclerk, the Duke of St Albans (1840–1898). The colliery proved to be extremely profitable, especially after the duke used his political influence to have a spur line connect it to the rail network. And then there was the coal: two shafts were sunk to a depth of 1,242 feet, and these gave access to the top-quality, six-foot-thick Top Hard coal seam; Bestwood was the first UK coal mine to produce a million tons of the stuff in a single year.

The ironworks closed in the 1920s, the colliery in 1967, but, remarkably, the pit's Victorian engine house and old winding gear have survived. The engine house is an attractive, vaguely Italianate structure of red brick with stone dressings; latticed beams connect it to the winding wheels. Inside is the only twin cylinder vertical steam engine to stand on its original site in the UK. The engine once lowered colliers into the mine shaft and winched mined coal to the surface; today, a glass-sided lift provides access to its several levels. The industrial sprawl and slag heaps that once surrounded the colliery have been turned into the Bestwood Country Park, with wooded parkland and walking trails.

Address Bestwood Colliery, Bestwood Country Park, Park Road, Bestwood Village, Nottingham, NG6 8TQ, +44 (0)115 975 7273, www.gedling.gov.uk | **Getting there** Tram to Butler's Hill, then a one-mile walk; alternatively, it's a six-mile drive north from central Nottingham | **Hours** Open access to Country Park; car park open Mon–Fri 8am–4pm, Sat & Sun dusk–dawn; Engine House Sat 10am–noon | **Tip** The owners of Bestwood Colliery built a village for their workers next to the pit in the 1870s. These terrace houses have survived with precious few exterior alterations, stringing out along Park Road, St Albans Road and The Square. On Park Road is the company's original headquarters: a heavy-duty, red-brick Victorian edifice with a clock tower that stands at the junction of Park Road and High Main Drive.

14 Birds Bakery

Eat like the locals – pork pie anyone?

If you want to discover what the average resident of Nottingham considers a gastronomic treat, visit Birds, whose neat and modern shops can be found right across the city. Still a family concern, Birds was founded in the neighbouring city of Derby in 1919 by three brothers, Frank, Thomas and Reginald. In 1951, it was passed on to two more Birds – another Reginald and Paul – who declared their ambition with refreshing simplicity: 'To provide our customers with the highest possible quality of cakes, pork pies, bread and savouries, at a reasonable cost and with a friendly and reliable service.' This proved a winning formula – and there are now over 60 outlets.

Birds offers a variety of popular sweet and savoury treats. You can choose a chunky sausage roll, a freshly-made-up roll (or 'cob' in the local dialect), a delicious mini-quiche or shiny teacake. Even more traditional are the tiny dishes of potted meat – sometimes called 'potted dog' hereabouts – and that's before you get to the oh-so sugary cakes. These range from trifles to custard tarts, cream and jam doughnuts, cream slices and puffs through to delicious apple pies – this author's favourite since they stopped making their tastebud-exploding blackcurrant pies.

Most Birds shops also sell 'Elephant's feet' – not, thank goodness, anything to do with the animal that never forgets, but a choux pastry bun filled with whipped cream and topped with chocolate – which do, of course, resemble, if rather vaguely, the aforesaid feet. Then there's a perennial favourite across the East Midlands, the pork pie, which consists of a compressed ball of meat encased in thick pastry. The traditional repast of the fox-hunting fraternity, the pork pie's popularity has spread far and wide, but it is something of an acquired taste, especially the jelly that fills the gap between the meat and the pastry.

Address There are numerous Birds outlets, but one of the most central is in the Victoria Shopping Centre, Lower Parliament Street, Nottingham, NG1 3QN, www.birdsbakery.com | **Getting there** Local bus (most lines) or tram to the city centre | **Hours** See website for current information on opening times | **Tip** All of the larger Birds outlets – including the one in the Victoria Centre and the one nearby at 25 Lister Gate – take pre-orders for party food from cakes and croissants to pork pies and quiches.

15 Birkin Building

From weaver to aristocrat in three generations

The architectural delights of the Lace Market, the city's most diverting quarter, reflect the roaring success of Nottingham's lace industry in the second half of the 19th century. The Adams Building (see ch. 4) is the single most impressive structure, but the most appealing streetscape is on Broadway, where a line of handsome, four-storey Victorian warehouses perform a delicate swerve as they march along the street.

The façades of these former lace warehouses are, for the most part, of reddish-orange brick trimmed with stone, but several have gone for a grander design, with dressed stone forming the entire ground floor. Amongst these, the most distinctive is the Birkin Building, which sports elaborate bay windows and a fancy carriage archway beneath a decorative scroll, all to a design by Thomas Chambers Hine (1813–1899), one of the city's most popular architects and himself the son of a hosiery manufacturer.

Finished in 1855, the Birkin Building was the headquarters of the eponymous, family-owned lace manufacturers. The Birkins started out as humble handloom weavers until the entrepreneurial Richard Birkin (1805–1870) took matters in hand, establishing a flourishing lace business in the 1820s. Over the course of the next 30 years, Richard became both extremely wealthy and a leading civic light, appointed as Lord Mayor of Nottingham on no fewer than three occasions.

His son, Thomas Birkin (1831–1922), reaped even greater rewards, expanding the business overseas and becoming a baronet: within three generations, the Birkins were thoroughly absorbed within the British establishment. There's one curious footnote: Thomas Birkin's granddaughter, Freda Dudley Ward (1894–1983), was the mistress of the Prince of Wales, later Edward VIII, for about a decade – an affair that Winston Churchill found to be 'quite pathetic'.

Address 2–12 Broadway, Nottingham, NG1 1PS | Getting there Local bus (most lines) or tram to the city centre, then a five-minute walk | Hours No entry, but façade visible at all times | Tip Nottingham's Victorian architects were keen to cash in on the building boom that created the Lace Market and the illustrious Watson Fothergill contributed with an imposing and dignified building near Broadway at the junction of Stoney Street and Barker Gate.

16 Boots the Chemist

Goose Gate start-up with a philanthropic edge

Boots, formerly Boots the Chemist, has a long association with Nottingham. It was here that the original Boot – John Boot (1815 – 1860) – set up shop, selling medicinal remedies before passing the business baton on to his wife, Mary, and their son, Jesse, who left school early to help his mother run the business.

Initially, the duo specialised in the sale of herbs, including roots, plants and flowers, which were collected locally before being dried and then powdered. Business boomed, and in the 1880s the Boots upgraded, establishing their first fully fledged store at 16 – 22 Goose Gate. A plaque commemorates this event and the building itself, with its wide windows and scroll-like columns, looks pretty much like it did when the Boots worked here. Jesse took over the sole running of the company in 1877, and proved to be a whizz as a businessman, developing inventive ways of selling his ever-expanding range of products. As a result, the opening of new stores went on apace: a flagship store was opened in Nottingham at 10 Pelham Street in 1892 – it still stands, but is now occupied by Zara – and 1933 saw the company's 1,000th store launched in Galashiels, Scotland.

Locally, Boots were renowned as paternalistic employers – with Boots sports grounds and social facilities notably well resourced. They also gave generously to local causes, even donating the land on which the University of Nottingham was to be built. They also diversified into manufacturing, and the company's local R&D department remains world class. The last Boot to run the company, John Boot (1889 – 1956), retired in 1953, since when the family's connection with the company has dissolved, prefiguring all sorts of corporate shenanigans that have disturbed the company's recent history. Nonetheless, Boots has retained its Nottingham base, and still employs over 6,000 people in and around the city.

Address 16–22 Goose Gate, Nottingham, NG1 1FF | Getting there Local bus (most lines) or tram to the city centre | Hours Always visible from outside | Tip Just up the slope and across the street from the old Boots premises is Ice Nine (www.icenine.co.uk), a curious sort of shop selling just about every sort of hippy/New Age/Goth bauble and trinket you can think of; it's been going since the 1970s, so it's something of an institution.

17 The Bottesford Witches

One earl, two children, three witches

The stroll down the path from the railway station into the heart of Bottesford is a delight, with the church of St Mary the Virgin standing in a loop of the River Devon, a rippling stream flanked by weeping willows and copper beeches. The setting is glorious, and so is the church's medieval steeple, which soars high above the parapets and pinnacles of the nave. Inside, it's the tombs of the chancel that catch the eye: after the Reformation, the Rutlands colonised the chancel and a gang of them are entombed here. They are large and imposing tombs for sure, but perhaps the most unusual is an Elizabethan alabaster extravagance in which the second earl and his wife are laid out beneath a dining table representing an altar.

The most interesting tomb is that of Francis Manners, 6th Earl of Rutland (1578–1632), shown with one wife slightly above, the other slightly below him. A wordy inscription extols the earl's virtues, and asserts that two of his children 'died in their infancy by wicked practises and sorcerye'; the children are at his feet, carrying skulls. Francis certainly believed their deaths were untoward, but quite why or how he fastened on three local women – Joan Flower and her daughters Margaret and Philippa – to accuse of witchcraft is impossible to say.

Predictably, given those superstitious times, the investigation the earl ordered stumbled into a stew of rumour and allegation, with the net of sorcery spreading out of control. In the event, Joan died on her way to trial, which at least gave a terrified Margaret the chance to blame her mother from the dock: Margaret said Joan had harmed the earl's son by stroking 'Rutterkin her cat [and familiar] with the boy's glove, after it was dipt in hot water'. The trial was the talk of the Jacobean court. Margaret was hanged, but Philippa managed to escape in mysterious circumstances: some thought she had bewitched her guards, others suggested she had drugged them.

Address St Mary the Virgin, Rectory Lane, Bottesford, Leicestershire, NG13 0DA, www.stmarysbottesford.co.uk | Getting there Train to Bottesford, then a five-minute walk; by car, it's an 18-mile drive from Nottingham to Bottesford via the A52 | Hours St Mary the Virgin open daily 9am–5pm | Tip For a coffee or a snack, make your way to *Venue 12 Café and Bar*, just a five-minute walk from St Mary, at 12 Queen Street (Mon–Fri 8.30am–3pm & Sat 10am–2pm).

18 Boulevard Works
Industrial architecture at its finest

Sitting tight against Radford Boulevard, a couple of miles to the north-west of the city centre, the Boulevard Works is one of the most impressive former tenement lace factories to have survived anywhere in the region, with well over 100 large windows rising in ranks to the top of its five-storey, red-brick frame. This lengthy façade barely registers any interruptions, but it is intercepted by several modest double-door entrances, one of which sports a stone lintel inscribed with the building's name.

The Boulevard Works was constructed in the 1880s – and extended in the 1890s – for Nottingham lace-makers George Henry Perry and Sons, who were keen to increase production. Good natural lighting was crucial in a lace factory, and consequently the windows seem almost overly large, though the trim blue-brick banding of the façade, as well as the curved window heads, polish things off very nicely. The works were designed to accommodate over 200 Leavers machines. Invented in Nottingham in 1813, these machines were improved on several occasions, and by the late 19th century they had become the most versatile way to manufacture patterned lace – and the city had a skilled workforce to keep them going.

How much Perry trusted the workers' punctuality is, however, a matter of debate as he purchased a large clock in 1894, and plonked it on top of the factory, high above the corner entrance. Precious little is known about George Henry Perry (1840 – 1927), never mind his workers, but his wife, Elizabeth (1842 – 1911), did have 10 children, two of whom died in infancy. One of their sons, Percy (1884 – 1916), joined the family business and then the army, where – as an officer in the Sherwood Foresters – he was unfortunate enough to be sent to Ireland to suppress the Easter Rising, where he was killed in action. The Boulevard Works is now student accommodation.

Address Boulevard Works, Radford Boulevard, Nottingham, NG7 5QJ | **Getting there** Bus along Alfreton Road to Hartley Road, then a five-minute walk | **Hours** Visible from outside only | **Tip** From the Boulevard Works, it's a 15-minute walk to Triumph Road. This was where Raleigh Bicycles had its main factory, but this was demolished in 2003 to be repaced by a series of super modern buildings that now comprise the University of Nottingham's Jubilee Campus. De-industralisation repaired?

19 Brian Clough Statue

He said he'd walked on the River Trent

Argumentative, awkward and brilliant, Brian Clough (1935 – 2004) was one of the finest football managers England has ever produced. Born in Middlesbrough, north-east England, he had been a prolific goal scorer, but his career was cut short on Boxing Day, 1962, when he was the victim of a particularly dreadful foul. Clough went on to learn his craft as a manager at Hartlepool in partnership with his best friend, Peter Taylor. They were a formidable duo – Clough with his distinctive man-management skills, Taylor as a scout with a canny eye for undeveloped talent. In 1967, the pair transferred to Derby County, where they won the First Division title, but thereafter Clough fell out with the Derby chairman and went to Leeds United, where his reign famously ended in uproar after just 44 days.

In 1975, Clough became manager of Nottingham Forest, where he stayed for the next 18 years, winning two European Cups and a basket full of trophies – including the 1977 – 1978 First Division title – with display after display of searing one-touch football. These were remarkable achievements, but they proved to be the high points of Clough's career and disappointments followed: in the early 1980s, Clough and Taylor quarrelled and never spoke again, and Clough was widely reported to be drinking heavily as his team faltered. Nonetheless, the people of Nottingham were loyal to the man, not least because of his unruly character and pithy sayings: 'I wouldn't say I was the best manager in the business, but I was in the top one.' Or, on what happened if a player disagreed with him: 'We talk about it for 20 minutes and then we decide I was right.'

Clough's simple and fetching statue was erected here in the centre of Nottingham by popular demand. The football stadium, the City Ground (see ch. 28), where he once held sway, lies a mile or so out of town by the River Trent.

Address King Street, Nottingham, NG1 2BH | Getting there Local bus (most lines) or tram to the city centre | Hours Open access; free | Tip The statue is a stone's throw from the Market Square, which was remodelled by a leading firm of landscape architects, Gustafson Porter, in 2007. Initially, many locals were not impressed by the change, but the design has proved to be popular in the long run.

20 Broadway Cinema

Comfortable seats and great films

Broadway Cinema is the cinematic focus of Nottingham, its screens showing a lively mix of art-house, indie and mainstream films. Much to their credit, they also vary the mix with special events such as live opera feeds from the Met in New York and 'Cult Horror Weekends'. Furthermore, Broadway has deeper local roots than you might perhaps expect.

It all began in the 1960s, with the establishment of the Nottingham Film Theatre inside these very premises, which was then the Co-operative Society Educational Centre. At the time, the Co-op had a progressive educational mission far beyond its supermarket role, and the Educational Centre was a handsome Modernist building adorned by mosaic-clad columns. The Nottingham Film Theatre soon established a solid reputation for the films it showed, and for many years it was the only place in Nottingham to show foreign films – apart, that is, from the seedy (and long gone) Moulin Rouge, which catered for a very different clientele, including, oddly enough, the Kray Twins, who are said to have popped up from London for a midnight screening of a 'blue movie' in 1966.

In the late 1980s, the Nottingham Film Theatre absorbed the Midland Group, a newer and more experimental cinematic venture, to become City Lights Cinema, which morphed into the Broadway Cinema in 1989. The new cinema was quick to declare its credentials, opening with *Enemies – A Love Story*, a strikingly original film by Paul Mazursky. Since then, the building has been remodelled several times. The number of screens has increased to four, and Broadway now sports an attractive and very distinctive glass façade.

Incidentally, before the Co-op took it over, this was the site of the Broad Street Wesley Chapel, where a young William Booth (see ch. 108) was converted to Christianity – hence the commemorative plaque of a heavily bearded Booth in the foyer.

Address 14–18 Broad Street, Nottingham, NG1 3AL, www.broadway.org.uk | Getting there Local bus (most lines) or tram to the city centre | Hours For show times visit cinema website | Tip Amongst the bevy of restaurants in the vicinity of Broadway Cinema, one of the best is Iberico World Tapas, a popular Spanish place in the old Shire Hall on High Pavement (www.ibericotapas.com).

21 Bromley House Library

A Georgian surprise

Tucked away behind the most inconsequential of doorways, right in the heart of the city, is Bromley House Library, one of the most interesting and captivating places in Nottingham. The library, along with its ground-floor walled garden, started out as a top-of-the-range Georgian town house built for George Smith, a wealthy banker, and his wife Mary, a direct descendant of James I.

Yet, things soon took a downward turn for the family: George's son – another George – enraged his wife with his neglect of her, but it was one of his servants who ruined George, accusing him of attempting to commit 'an unnatural act'. George was tried, found guilty and imprisoned, and by 1810 the house lay empty and neglected. It was then that a group of gentlemen pooled their resources to establish what has gradually evolved into Bromley House Library, which is still going strong as a (private) subscription library, though its membership rates are very reasonable. Entry to the library is via a wide flight of stairs decorated with portraits of assorted gentlemen. Pride of place goes to a (rather dusty) painting of the 1st Duke of Richmond, one of Charles II's many illegitimate children, who is decked out in his glad rags from big wig down to dinky high heels.

Beyond is the main floor, where the front room is infinitely reassuring with its bookcases rising up to the fancy decorative plasterwork of the ceiling, whilst the overmantel of the old fireplace sports a romanticised painting of Clifton Grove as of 1822 by Rawson Walker (1796 – 1873). A Nottingham man, Walker made a tidy living from his classical landscape paintings. On the same floor, flanked by more bookcases, a delightful, self-supporting (if somewhat creaky) spiral staircase, dating from 1857, climbs to an upper-level gallery with matching balusters and more rooms – and many, more books, some of which are extremely old.

Address Angel Row, Nottingham, NG1 6HL, +44 (0)115 947 3134,
www.bromleyhouse.org, enquiries@bromleyhouse.org | Getting there Local bus (most lines)
or tram to the city centre | Hours Mon–Fri 9.30am–5pm, Wed till 7pm, Sat 9.30am–4pm.
Note that Bromley House is unable to accommodate ad hoc visits. Please call or email
ahead of time to arrange a tour or visit. | Tip After a lengthy period of closure, Nottingham
Central Library (www.nottinghamcitylibraries.co.uk) has reopened in smart new premises
down in the Broad Marsh.

22 By Our Hands…

Nottingham's woodworking co-operative

Sneinton Market, on the east side of the city centre, has become something of an artsy-creative hub since the Art Deco buildings of the former fruit and vegetable market were spruced up in the 2010s. It's here you'll find a hatful of small businesses mostly with an alternative vibe – from cake makers through to textile shops – but one of the most unusual, By Our Hands, We Make our Way, is not commercial at all, but rather an assertion of a different way of life. The founder, the clear-sighted Martin Sommerville, attempts to summarise it as being about 'intentional living, building a sense of community' primarily through the medium of woodworking.

The interior of By Our Hands, We Make Our Wayis simply charming. The sweet smell of wood envelopes a jingle jangle of tools and work benches, lockers and a sofa, all set amidst a miscellany of little wooden sculptures left behind by previous woodworkers. If you're already good with wood, you can come in, use the tools and work under your own direction, butBy Our Hands also offers an exemplary range of woodworking courses, from stool making and spoon carving through to relief carving and woodblock printmaking – all at minimal cost. Neither are other conveniences forgotten – there's coffee and tea, dates and biscuits.

One particular highlight is the co-operative's Green Woodworking workshops, in which participants learn how to work with the grain of freshly cut trees; another is thepopular Family Workshops, during which, as you might expect from the name, families tackle a project of their own, working at their own pace with tools and workbenches provided; Martin oversees it all, adding ideas and practical assistance as required. As someone who spent two years at school trying to make a dovetail joint, this author appreciated one of Martin's workplace mottos about 'Forgetting failure and finding joy'.

Address Unit 42 & 43, Sneinton Market, Nottingham, NG1 1DQ, +44 (0)7496 680507, www.wemakeourway.co.uk | **Getting there** Local bus (most lines) or tram to the city centre, then a five-minute walk | **Hours** Opening hours vary depending on the programme of workshops, etc; please check website | **Tip** From By Our Hands, it's just a hop, skip and jump to a relaxed and fashionable café, Blend (www.blendnottingham.co.uk).

23 — Byron at Newstead Abbey

Where Byron dipped his quill

The main house at Newstead Abbey is a curious, maze-like affair reflecting its complicated history. Parts of the house date back to the time – before the Reformation – when this was a priory, but mostly the house reflects the assorted endeavours of a trio of 19th-century owners, easily the most famous of whom is the celebrated poet Lord Byron (1788–1824), who inherited a ruinous Newstead Abbey in 1809.

Byron lived here for nine years, but could not afford to refurbish more than a handful of rooms, the first of which – on the self-guided tour – is the Dining Room, a cosy, wood-panelled affair with an ornate fireplace. Moving on, the Library was a ruin in Byron's time – it was restored by the next owner, Thomas Wildman (1787–1859) – but it's here you'll find a charming selection of Byron mementoes. Amongst much else, there are his walnut and silver pistols, his boxing gloves, and the extravagant cavalry helmet with a protruding (phallic) black crest that Byron had made for himself in Genoa. This vainglorious helmet – no-one ever accused Byron of modesty – was in preparation for the poet's departure for Greece, where he went to fight the Turks in the Greek war of independence. Frankly, Byron didn't prove much use militarily, but his death at Missolonghi helped advertise the justness of their cause.

Near the Library is Byron's bedroom, with its four-poster bed, then it's on to the Grand Drawing Room, once the monastic refectory but lavishly restored by Wildman, the cost covered by the profits from his family's sugar plantation. Near the end of the tour come the cloisters, partly Victorian and partly medieval, and the Gothic Revival chapel with its colourful stencilling, intricate tiling and stained-glass windows. The latter was created for William (1829–1899) and Emilia (1844–1889) Webb, who bought Newstead in 1861, initiating its Victorian heyday.

Byron's boxing gloves, made of buff leather. Byron was a strong boxer and a follower of that sport. When in residence at Newstead Abbey he trained in the Great Dining Room (now the Great Drawing Room). This and the Great Hall, the two largest chambers in the house, he reserved for his sporting activities.

NA 309

Address Ravenshead, Nottinghamshire, NG15 9HJ, +44 (0)115 876 3100, www.newsteadabbey.org.uk | Getting there Regular buses from the city centre drop passengers at the gatehouse beside the A 60, from where it's a 25-minute walk to the house; by car, it's an 11-mile drive from Nottingham to the Abbey. | Hours Sat & Sun 11am–4pm | Tip Byron and his daughter, the mathematician Ada Lovelace, are interred in the Byron vault, at St Mary Magdalene church, Marketplace, Hucknall, NG15 7AS, www.hucknallparishchurch.org.uk; Hucknall, a former colliery town, is five miles south of Newstead Abbey.

24 Castle Rock Brewery

Taste the beers of a local brewery

The revival of British beer brewing over the last 30 years has been a wonder to behold, and Nottingham has joined in the boozy bonanza, now boasting a hatful of small breweries. In a well-told and well-known local tale, Chris Holmes can lay claim to kick-starting this beer revival in Nottinghamshire, opening his own pub just outside the city in 1977.

Holmes, who had been chair of CAMRA (the Campaign for Real Ale), knew what he was about and, flouting the monopolistic brewers of the day, installed a row of hand pumps in his pub to dispense real ale. This proved to be a great success, and the company Holmes founded subsequently grew by leaps and bounds. Today, several of the best pubs in the city and its environs are owned and operated by his company, now called Castle Rock. All are committed to selling cask beers from a variety of brewers, though pride of place mostly goes to the beverages produced by the company itself – they started brewing their own beers from premises near Nottingham railway station in 1997. The brewers at Castle Rock have proved to be an inventive lot, but perhaps their greatest success is the award-winning blonde beer, Harvest Pale: at 3.8%, this is described as having a 'delicate citrus character', and remains a real favourite. For something stronger, you might try the really very tasty, amber-coloured Preservation, at 4.4%.

Perhaps the most agreeable Castle Rock pub in Nottingham is the Lincolnshire Poacher, a traditional, beer-lovers' sort of place with a long, L-shaped bar at the front, and a neat little, wood-panelled snug behind. To the rear is a more modern, conservatory-like extension, as well as outdoor mini-shelters which extend into the walled back yard. The pub offers a wide variety of cask and keg ales, including, of course, Castle Rock brews, plus a liver-threatening number of malt whiskeys.

Address The Lincolnshire Poacher, 161-163 Mansfield Road, Nottingham, NG1 3FR, +44 (0)115 941 1584, www.castlerockbrewery.co.uk | Getting there Local bus (most lines) or tram to the city centre, then a 5- to 10-minute walk | Hours Mon noon–10pm, Tue–Sun noon–11pm | Tip The most central Castle Rock pub is The Castle (www.thecastlenottingham.co.uk), which occupies a rambling old building directly opposite the castle at 1 Castle Road. The building has all the hallmarks of a Watson Fothergill confection – from its irregular roof lines to its subtle patterned brickwork.

25 Castle Wharf

Canalside jauntiness

For a brief period from around the 1790s, thousands of navvies were digging canals in what must have seemed like every corner of the land. Nottingham was no exception, but the situation here was complicated. The city was within easy striking distance of the River Trent, but only at a point where navigation just upstream was problematic. After much toing-and-froing, the end result was that one company built the Nottingham Canal from the city to a point below the difficult part of the river, while another constructed the so-called Beeston Cut, to bypass that same stretch of the Trent; the two canals met at Lenton, just to the west of the city, where the owners of the Cut installed a chain to prevent boats from passing from one to the other without paying a toll.

In the event, the railways were soon to undercut the canals and only parts of this watery network are still in use – principally the loop from the Meadow Lane lock, near Trent Bridge, to the Beeston Lock to the south-west of the city centre. This loop, now the Nottingham & Beeston Canal, slips through the heart of Nottingham at Castle Wharf, where concerted efforts have been made to create a waterfront vibe. It's been a successful venture.

The wharf's key note building is the former British Waterways warehouse, a six-storey block of 1919, whose paired windows and top-to-bottom loading bays catch the eye. Around and about are bits of the old, including a hump-back bridge, a couple of old jetties, a warehouse or two and the Castle Lock, as well as some clever reinventions: the Victorian building that once housed Fellows, Morton & Clayton, a major player in canal transportation, has, for instance, been turned into a pub. There's a lot of modern stuff too, but care has been taken to make the more recent buildings sympathetic with their surroundings. The pubs on the wharf buzz and hum at night.

Address Castle Wharf, Nottingham, NG1 7AU | Getting there Local bus (most lines) or tram to city centre, then an eight-minute walk | Hours Always accessible | Tip You can walk or cycle in either direction along the canal from Castle Wharf. On foot, it takes about 20 minutes to reach City Ground, the home of Nottingham Forest (see ch. 28) and the site of Trent Bridge Cricket Ground (see ch. 101).

26 Chilwell Explosion Memorial

The blast was heard over 20 miles away

It was World War I that transformed Chilwell, previously an inconsequential village five miles south-west of Nottingham. In 1915, there was a desperate shortage of artillery shells for the British army, and so the splendidly named Viscount Godfrey Chetwynd (1863–1936) was dispatched to sort things out.

A dynamic man, Chetwynd happened upon Chilwell, which had two main advantages for producing shells: it was flat, which made the construction of a factory straightforward, and there were hundreds of (under-employed) textile workers in nearby Nottingham. As managing director, Chetwynd soon had an enormous shell-filling factory in production, employing some 7,000 workers, around a third of whom were women. It was here, in what was officially National Shell Filling Factory No. 6, that the workers primed artillery shells by fitting detonators and filling them with a highly explosive compound called Amatol. This was obviously a dangerous job, during which the chemicals turned the women's skin yellow – hence the nickname 'Canary Girls'.

Over the course of the war, the factory churned out over 19 million shells, but this achievement was dimmed and dented by the events of 1 July, 1918, when there was a huge explosion in the factory – a catastrophe that killed 134, and injured nearly 300. One eyewitness described people with 'their faces black and charred, some bleeding with limbs torn off'.

Given war-time censorship, the explosion was heavily under-reported, but there was an investigation. Chetwynd blamed sabotage, but it seems more likely that lax safety regulations combined with overly ambitious production targets were the cause. Many of the bodies were unidentifiable and these were interred in a mass grave in the graveyard at St Mary's Church, where they are commemorated by a blue plaque.

THE CHILWELL
EXPLOSION

On 1st July 1918 an explosion
destroyed part of the
Chilwell Shell Filling Factory
killing 139 workers.

Many of the victims are
buried in these graves.

Address St Mary's Church, Church Lane, Attenborough, Beeston, Nottingham, NG9 6AS, www.attenboroughchurch.org.uk | **Getting there** Train to Attenborough, then a five-minute walk | **Hours** The mass grave and blue plaque have open access; church open Mon, Wed & Fri 9am–1pm, Tue & Thu 10am–11am | **Tip** The old and handsome house next door to St Mary's Church was the birthplace of the Parliamentary leader and regicide Henry Ireton (1611–1651) – hence the plaque. A large pyramidal monument was erected to commemorate the Chilwell dead in 1919; it still survives, but it's located inside Chilwell's Chetwynd barracks, which are not currently open to the public, though that is likely to change in the future.

27 — Chocolate Utopia
Mouth-watering handmade chocolates

Leading off from the Market Square, Friar Lane takes its name from a Carmelite Friary that once stood here, but the monks are long gone and today this is one of Nottingham's more agreeable streets, its lower reaches framed by several attractive 1950s buildings. About half-way up, in neat and trim premises, you'll find an outstanding chocolatier – Chocolate Utopia. An independent, family-owned business, established in 2004 by Chris and Helen Forster, they make their chocolates on the premises, both out of sight in the basement and at the back of the shop, where you can observe them in full chocolatey action. They seem to have chocolate in their veins: Helen's parents once ran a chocolate shop in York.

Chris and Helen only make chocolates they like themselves – they don't do lavender or violet-infused chocolates, for example – but this is hardly a hardship, as their range of tasty chocs is truly lip-smacking: there are 10 different types of truffle, pralines, 'Dutch gold' (with advocaat cream in dark chocolate), Morello cherry chocolates, Brazil nuts encased in chocolate and, this author's favourite, the Malibu – light coconut with rum cream covered with two types of chocolate. The chocolates, which can be purchased in several box sizes, are neatly displayed in the shop's glass cabinet, or you can settle down for a longer stay: there are a couple of chairs at the front of the shop where visitors can savour their super-thick, super-rich hot chocolate.

They are also open to individual customer requests – for example they'll produce handmade Easter eggs with specific dedications, although you'll need to order well in advance. As you might anticipate, locals regularly post rave reviews all over the internet – and it's even alleged that some people only come to Nottingham to buy their exquisite creations, but obviously that just can't be true. Who could possibly be the source of this calumny?

Address 30 Friar Lane, Nottingham, NG1 6DQ, +44 (0)115 947 0016, www.chocolate-utopia.co.uk | Getting there Local bus (most lines) or tram to the city centre, then a three-minute walk | Hours Tue – Sat 10am – 5.30pm | Tip Nottingham is lucky to have two great chocolatiers, Chocolate Utopia and Luisa's, a vegan chocolatier down in Sneinton Market (see ch. 53).

28 City Ground

Can Nottingham Forest ever be champions again?

Home to Nottingham Forest Football Club (NFFC) since 1898, the City Ground sits tight beside the River Trent, a 20-minute walk from Nottingham railway station. Since the halcyon days of its finest manager, Brian Clough (see ch. 19), who led the precious club to two European Cups in 1979 and 1980, there has been little for fans to cheer about. At time of writing, Forest (aka The Reds or The Tricky Trees) are struggling to survive amongst the giants of English football in the Premier League.

Few would argue that the City Ground, with a capacity of just over 30,000, is one of England's more appealing football stadiums, cauldron-like on big-match days, but perhaps at its most atmospheric in the dark days of winter, when supporters stream along the riverside walkway amidst the mists that spin off the river. It's actually something of a miracle that the ground has survived at all. Time and again, it has dodged efforts to close it down and move Forest to one of those purpose-built stadiums so beloved of developers, regardless that these are often in the middle of nowhere – Derby's move from the Baseball Ground to Pride Park in 1997 being a case in point. There have been squabbles about the existing location too. Nottingham City Council, which owns the land, fell out with Forest over the club's plans to extend the stadium in the early 1990s. To thwart Forest, it's said that the Council demanded an enormous rental for the 8-15m strip of land separating the stadium from the river – a so-called 'ransom strip'; fortunately, cool heads prevailed and the riverside strip survives.

Football club owners do, of course, come and go, but Evangelos Marinakis, the Greek shipping magnate who bought the club in 2017, seems committed to Forest. He has spent millions on transfer fees, initiated plans to improve the stadium, and signed a 250-year extension of the lease on the City Ground.

Address West Bridgford, Nottingham, NG2 5FJ, +44 (0)115 982 4388, www.nottinghamforest.co.uk | Getting there Frequent buses to the City Ground from several stops in the city centre, Angel Row included; alternatively, if you're feeling energetic, it's a 30-minute walk. | Hours See website for details of regular guided tours | Tip For lovers of football trivia, the 1878 match between Nottingham Forest and Sheffield was the first time a referee used a whistle; City Ground is only a five minutes' walk from Meadow Lane (see ch. 56), the home ground of Nottingham's second professional football team, Notts County.

29 __ Clipstone Headstocks
Industrial architecture at its most imposing

Gaunt reminders of a lost industry, the winding-gear – or head-stocks – of the old Clipstone Colliery soar high above their surroundings, some 18 miles north of Nottingham.Clipstone pit was opened in 1922, but its best years came after nationalisation in 1947, when the National Coal Board invested heavily, bringing extra coal seams within reach as shafts were sunk down to around 1,000 yards. The board also installed improved winding gear in 1953 – and this is what you see today.

In 1986, Clipstone produced no less than a million tons of coal – enough, you would have thought, to secure its future, but this was not the case: the colliery was mothballed just seven years later, and closed in 2003. Even worse, there was little the miners could do as the National Union of Mineworkers (NUM), which had opposed pit closures in the Miners' Strike of 1984-5, had been crushed by Margaret Thatcher's government. For a variety of reasons, most Notts miners worked during the strike, but if they thought the Conservatives would reward them by not closing their pits, they were mistaken, and the county's last colliery closed in 2015.

Considering there were once around 30 pits in Nottinghamshire, employing around 30,000 miners, there are surprisingly few visible reminders of the coal industry: the slag heaps have been grassed over and most of the pit heads are long gone, so Clipstone's headstocks are something of a rarity, especially as, at over 200 feet high, they are the tallest in Europe. A Grade II listing now gives the headstocks protection as it does to the key contents of the large industrial building at their base, principally the surviving winding machinery, power house and motor generator room. It's currently not possible to enter – the headstocks are fenced off – but there are plans to turn the complex into a leisure centre, so the future looks more promising.

Address Mansfield Road, Clipstone, Nottinghamshire, NG21 9EH | Getting there Clipstone Colliery Headstocks are beside the B 6030 in Clipstone village, some 18 miles from Nottingham | Hours Not currently accessible | Tip The old slag heaps just to the southwest of the Clipstone Headstocks have been returned to nature and patterned with footpaths. The Vicar Water Viewpoint offers wide views over the whole area.

30 Colston Bassett

Historic village with a fine country pub

The easy rolling landscapes of the Nottinghamshire Wolds fill out the south-east corner of the county, and it's here, some 11 miles from Nottingham, you'll find the prosperous village of Colston Bassett, which dates back to Saxon times, if not before. Colston Bassett may seem serene and tranquil today, but it has something of a bumpy history. In 1604, it was devastated by an outbreak of the bubonic plague – so much so that it was actually quarantined: so-called 'plague stones' were positioned on the edge of the village in order that incoming necessities could be placed there in exchange for money, disinfected in vinegar.

A few decades later and the local gentry was bitterly divided between Royalists and Parliamentarians. Colston Bassett's Colonel Francis Hacker chose the latter, becoming a respected and incorruptible cavalry commander and associate of John Hutchinson of neighbouring Owthorpe (see ch. 92). It was Hacker's involvement in the execution of Charles I that was to be his undoing: he commanded the halberdiers who escorted the king to and from his trial, and as a consequence he was executed at the Restoration – a fate to which he seems to have been resigned.

Today, a village cross, raised to celebrate the accession of William IV in 1830, stands at Colston Bassett's main crossroads. From here it's the briefest of strolls to the Martins Arms, which occupies ancient premises that once served as a combined farm and ale house. The interior, with its wooden beams, antique furniture and open fireplaces, is infinitely cosy and the food is simply superb – modern British cuisine at its very best, from the monk fish wrapped in scampi fries and roast leg of lamb with red cabbage through to mouth-watering desserts such as baked advocaat cheesecake and raspberry and peach puddings. In the summer, as an added bonus, you can eat and drink outside in the garden.

Address Martins Arms, School Lane, Colston Bassett, Nottingham, NG12 3FD, +44 (0)1949 730106, www.themartinsarms.co.uk | Getting there No direct buses; around 30 minutes by car from Nottingham | Hours Mon–Thu noon–9.30pm, Fri & Sat noon–11pm & Sun noon–7pm; kitchen: Mon–Fri 12.30–2pm & 5.30–9pm, Sat 12.30–9pm & Sun 12.30–5pm | Tip Stilton, a cheese with its own PDO (Protected Designation of Origin), can only be made in this part of the East Midlands, and it's on sale in the village at Colston Bassett Dairy (www.colstonbassettdairy.co.uk).

31 Council House Lions

Left Lion time…

In the middle of Nottingham is the Market Square, a handsome, airy piazza flanked by an attractive medley of old and new buildings of various dates and styles. The site of public marches and demonstrations, not to mention an artificial sandy beach in summer, the Market Square's pre-eminent building is the imposing Council House (town hall), a handsome Neo-Baroque structure built as part of a make-work scheme that employed hundreds of men during the Great Depression of the late 1920s.

The building's grand façade comprises eight stone columns set beneath a tympanum decorated with symbolic figures such as Justice, with a mighty domed clock tower rising high above. Nikolaus Pevsner was very sniffy about the place in his 1951 survey of Nottinghamshire: 'Not much can be said in defence of this kind of neo-Baroque display,' he moaned. Yet locals are extremely fond of their Council House – or at least they are of the two Art Deco lions that stand guard outside – Oscar on the right, and Leo on the left. To the casual visitor, the two heavyweight beasties may seem fairly routine, but to Nottingham folk mention of the Left Lion will almost always bring a smile: for no obvious reason, the Left Lion has long been *the place* to meet, especially for a first date, creating a veritable scrum of anticipation and desire amidst a cloud of perfume and aftershave. Incidentally, the architect responsible for the lions named them 'Agamemnon' and 'Menelaus' – but Nottingham folk were having none of that.

As a final bonus, the belfry tower of the Council House is home to 'Little John', supposedly the deepest-toned clock bell in the country. The bell weighs over 10 tonnes, and its infinitely reassuring and immediately recognisable strike can be heard for a distance of around eight miles. Little John was, of course, the bosom chum of Robin Hood.

Address Market Square, Nottingham, NG1 2DT, www.nottinghamcity.gov.uk/council-house | **Getting there** Local bus (most lines) and tram to the city centre | **Hours** Market Square and Lions – open access. Council House opening hours vary – see website for current information on visiting | **Tip** Down an alley near the Council House is Five Leaves (www.fiveleavesbookshop.co.uk), an independent, radical bookshop of some national renown. Amongst much else, they offer an extensive programme of lectures, meetings and readings.

32 Cranmer's Mound

Aslockton: shadows of a martyred archbishop

To every reader of Hilary Mantel's *Wolf Hall* trilogy, the figure of Thomas Cranmer (1489–1556), one-time Archbishop of Canterbury, will be very familiar. Mantel fixes this redoubtable character firmly in her historical gaze when he was at the height of his powers, but Cranmer's origins were modest, born the son of minor gentry in the village of Aslockton, to the east of Nottingham.

There are several reminders of Cranmer in the village today, including the names of a school, a pub and the village hall, but the most intriguing is Cranmer's Mound, a grassy conical hump located just a four-minute walk from the village's Main Street. The mound concerned started out as the motte (raised earthworks) of a small Norman stronghold complete with a tower and a ditch, but by Cranmer's time it was mainly used as a viewing platform – or prospect mound – overlooking a network of fish ponds. Local legend asserts that Cranmer returned to Aslockton when he was archbishop to visit his brother, and it was then that he clambered up the mound not for the fish, but to listen to the bells of a nearby church.

True or not, the name stuck, though it's perhaps more likely that Cranmer's martyrdom ensured the survival of the name rather than a casual visit. During the reigns of Henry VIII and Edward VI, Cranmer played a crucial role in pushing through the Protestant Reformation, but he was in trouble as soon as the very Catholic Mary Tudor became queen in 1553. As it turned out, Mary had Cranmer imprisoned and interrogated under charges of treason and heresy in a bitter battle of religious wills. Cranmer made several recantations, but these failed to save him from being condemned to death as a heretic as Mary felt he was just too visible a symbol of Protestantism to be spared. Finally, after calling the pope the Antichrist, he was led to the stake, famously plunging his right hand into the heart of the flames as symbolic punishment for it signing his earlier recantations.

Address Cranmer's Mound, off Main Street, Aslockton, Nottinghamshire, NG13 9AL |
Getting there Train to Aslockton, then a five-minute walk; by car, via the A 52 (13 miles) |
Hours Open access during daylight hours | Tip From Main Street, it takes around five
minutes to reach Cranmer's Mound via the signed public footpath that begins in between
Saucer Farm and the Thomas Cranmer Centre. It's a pleasant journey by train from
Aslockton to Newark, whose several enjoyable attractions include its castle (see ch. 62).

33 Daily Express Building

Victorian building with literary connections

There was a time, not so long ago, when every self-regarding book-case carried at least one novel by the English author Graham Greene (1904–1991). Those days may have gone, but Greene's subtle thrillers, with their moral and political complexities, retain an enduring appeal, none more so than *Brighton Rock*. In 1925, the young Graham Greene washed up here in Nottingham as a junior editor at the Nottingham Journal. The premises the Journal occupied were actually those of its predecessor, the Nottingham Daily Express, a liberal newspaper that wore its political affiliations on its sleeve: in the 1870s, they had asked the prolific architect Watson Fothergill (see ch. 104) to design their offices; the end result was a real Victorian extravagance, which comes complete with a round corner tower supported by slender columns, and adorned by decorative stonework.

In recent years, this handsome building has struggled to find a vocation – the ground floor now accommodates a Tesco mini-super-market – but the corner tower has survived in good condition, its recessed entrance adorned by the heads of three prominent Liberal politicians – Richard Cobden, John Bright and William Gladstone – just as the owners of the Nottingham Daily Express had ordained.

It's fair to say that Greene liked the newspaper's premises, but was far from enamoured by his job – he snootily moaned that it was a 'third-rate paper, run by third-rate people'. Neither did he take to Nottingham, a working-class city where the thoroughly middle-class Greene felt ill at ease. Nonetheless, it was here that he picked up the Catholicism that so permeated his later work, strolling over to St Barnabas, the city's Catholic cathedral (see ch. 91), to be received into the faith in 1926. After four months or so, Greene was off, proclaiming – really rather unfairly – 'Thank God Nottingham's over'.

Address 19–20 Upper Parliament Street, Nottingham, NG1 2AQ | Getting there Local bus (most lines) or tram to the city centre | Hours Façade visible at all times | Tip The bright-white, four-storey building just two doors up from the Daily Express Building began as the Elite Cinema in the early 1920s. Its cinematic days are long gone, but its striking faience frontage has survived and reflects the spirit of the times with the Elite built to resemble the grand movie palaces that were springing up all over America.

34 Danish Homestore

Danish design enhances everyday life

If you have a taste for Danish design, you should hot foot it to the Danish Homestore – it's simply fabulous. Here you'll find an outstanding selection of vintage Danish furniture, displayed over a mini-maze of rooms that spread over three large floors, in a big old building beside one of the city's main streets. There are chairs and tables, sofas and settees, as well as mirrors, bookcases, desks and chests of drawers. As you might expect, it's all for sale, so what you see varies from week to week, even day to day, but there's always something to catch the eye.

When this author last popped in, the prime exhibits were two rare 1940s Danish bucket chairs, upholstered in Alpaca wool – £12,000 the pair admittedly, but worth every penny of someone's money. Rather more affordable was the wide selection of lovely, angular Danish dining tables, complete with wooden plug joints and exquisite grained wood, often in oak, teak and rosewood. There's real demand for Danish furniture, whose sleek designs and high quality are so appealing, so don't necessarily expect any amazing bargains – but bargains there often are, and the shop certainly doesn't waste money prettifying the interior of the building, whose rooms are agreeably dishevelled.

As another plus, Danish Homestore remains a family business. It was founded in the mid-1980s by Roger Harrison, but is now run by his affable son, Simon, whose expert eye oversees the import of vintage and second-hand furniture direct from Denmark. There are prime pieces from the 1940s onwards and, if you're lucky, you'll spot furniture from the likes of Finn Juhl and Hans Wegner, Illum Wikkelso and Niels Koefoed. Naturally enough, not all of Simon's purchases are in prime condition, but this isn't a problem, as Danish Homestore has a large workshop, where each piece is thoroughly cleaned and restored as required.

Address 88–94 Derby Road, Nottingham, NG1 5FD, +44 (0)7512 781977, www.danish-homestore.com | Getting there Local bus (most lines) or tram to the city centre, then a 5- to 10-minute walk up along Derby Road | Hours Mon–Wed, Fri & Sat 10am–5pm | Tip If you're thinking of splashing out on a piece of Danish furniture, you might chew over your options at The Sir John Borlase Warren, an agreeable pub on Canning Circus, a short walk away up Derby Road.

35 Edwin Starr's Grave

War – what is it good for? Absolutely nothing…

Wilford Hill (Southern) Cemetery and Crematorium, around four miles south of the city centre, has been used for burials since 1919 and cremations since 1931. It occupies a large and grassy site that slopes up to the brow of a hill, where you'll find a desultory-looking stone chapel. Many a Nottingham lad and lass has been interred here, but only one American soul singer: Charles Edwin Hatcher, better known as Edwin Starr (1942–2003). Born in Nashville, Starr moved to Detroit as a young man. It was there that he signed with Ric-Tic Records, and with whom, in 1966, he recorded his first major hit, the inventive 'S.O.S.' (Stop Her On Sight).

In the meantime, Barry Gordy of (Tamla) Motown fame had become uneasy at the success of Ric-Tic Records so, in 1968, he did the sensible thing and bought the company lock, stock and barrel – including its artists. It was to be with Motown that Starr notched up his biggest international hits, firstly the foot-stomping soul classic '25 Miles' (1969) and then, modifying his style, a strident and intense funk version of 'War' (1970), aimed against the Vietnam War. It has become one of the most popular protest songs ever recorded. 'War' was to be the last of Starr's major hits, though he did record a string of moderately successful songs throughout the 1970s and 1980s, mixing styles – including disco – and appearing on a hatful of different record labels.

Starr moved to England in the early 1980s, at least partly because of his popularity on the northern soul scene. Indeed, his gravestone is inscribed with 'Our Agent 00 Soul'. When he died, he was living in Bramcote, a Nottingham suburb. Local legend has it that when a journalist telephoned his family to ask how and why Starr had ended up here, he was told the singer couldn't afford a house in Wollaton, the suburb next door – not quite the kind of reason he was expecting.

Address Wilford Hill (Southern) Cemetery, Loughborough Road, Nottingham, NG2 7FE, www.nottinghamcity.gov.uk | **Getting there** Bus to Wilford Hill (Southern) Cemetery. To find Starr's grave, proceed up the path to the main (stone) chapel and it's on the right, around 100 yards away – past 13 or 14 rows of tombs and behind a clump of three smallish evergreens. | **Hours** Jan–Feb & Nov–Dec Mon–Sat 8am–4pm & Sun 9am–4pm; Mar & Oct Mon–Sat 8am–5pm & Sun 9am–5pm; Apr–Sep Mon–Sat 8am–6pm & Sun 9am–6pm | **Tip** It would be easy to spend an hour or two wandering the cemetery. Some of the more recent graves are exercises in exuberance, whereas all is sombre restraint in that section maintained by the Commonwealth War Graves Commission – beside the distinctive Portland stone Cross of Sacrifice; around 200 military personnel are buried here.

36 Felley Priory

Exquisite gardens and a lovely tea room

Nestled in a gentle, wooded valley, Felley Priory is a delight. Monks were the first people to make their mark here, but the priory they established in 1156 played second fiddle to the larger abbey over at Newstead (see ch. 23). During the Reformation, the estate passed into the hands of the local gentry – the Millington family – and the (private) house you see today, with its distinctive line of elongated chimneys, mostly dates from this period, though bits and pieces were incorporated from the priory.

The most notable resident was Gilbert Millington (1598–1666), a radical lawyer and MP, who supported Parliament during the Civil War, and signed the warrant for the execution of Charles I. As a regicide, Millington was liable to be put to death at the Restoration, but by accident rather than design he managed to avoid this fate, being sentenced to life imprisonment instead – unlike his ally Francis Hacker, from Colston Bassett (see ch. 30).

In the 1970s, the owners of Felley Priory, the Chaworth-Musters, turned their attention to the gardens – and these, covering 2.5 acres, are simply gorgeous. The priory is 600ft above sea level, hence the yew hedges, and in spring time the orchard is carpeted with a sea of daffodils, whilst magnolias and snake's head fritillary underplant the trees in the specimen shrubbery area.

In the summer, attention moves to both the herbaceous borders and the walled rose garden, and everywhere there's topiary, with bushes fashioned into peacocks, swans and so on. The topiary provided the original framework on which the garden was shaped, and in winter, when things die back, it becomes the gardens' outstanding feature. After the gardens, you can drop by the nursery and pop into the tea room, which serves the tastiest of light meals, ranging from crumpets and croissants through to the freshest of sandwiches.

Address Underwood, Nottingham, NG16 5FJ, +44 (0)1773 810230, www.felleypriory.co.uk | **Getting there** By car, around 30 minutes north-west of Nottingham via the A610/M1 | **Hours** Gardens and nursery Tue–Fri 9am–4pm; tea room Tue–Fri 10am–4pm, no public access to house | **Tip** From Felley Priory, it's just four miles south to the town of Eastwood, where you'll find the mildly diverting D H Lawrence Birthplace Museum (www.broxtowe.gov.uk), in an old terraced house at 8A Victoria Street.

37 __ The Forest

A welcome splash of greenery in a busy city

The Forest – or more properly The Forest Recreation Ground – is a large open space located just north of the city centre. Once the southern-most portion of Sherwood Forest, it seemed likely that this chunk of land would be swallowed up by the city, but the council took matters in hand, securing, in 1845, an enclosure act that protected it in perpetuity. Thereafter, the Victorians hired the landscape gardener Joseph Paxton to flush out a design. Paxton respected the Forest's contours, and the network of footpaths he laid out has pretty much survived to this day.

The southern portion of the Forest occupies a steep, lightly wooded ridge, which is separated from the fields below by a wide and elegant walkway. The eastern end of the walkway is occupied by the sweet little Forest Lodge, a neo-classical structure of 1857, that has seen service as a Police Station – hence the basement cell. The flat, grassy fields on the north side of the Forest have long been popular for all sorts of sports, but originally, in the 18th century, it was horse racing and cock fighting that dominated the calendar, attracting huge and unruly crowds. The centre of the action was a large grandstand, but this was knocked down long ago with today's trim pavilion being its only successor.

The Forest is at its busiest during Goose Fair, Nottingham's largest annual event. The fair dates back to at least the 14th century, and was held in the Market Square until it moved to the Forest in 1928. For most of its history, the Fair was a major livestock market, named after the geese herded here from the Lincolnshire fens. Nowadays, it's all gimcrackery – from white-knuckle rides, carousels and dodgems through to cuddly toys and candy floss. The Fair takes place during the first week of October. Traditionally lasting five days, it has recently been extended to ten, which perhaps takes away some of its special atmosphere and character.

Address Gregory Boulevard, Nottingham, NG7 6HB | **Getting there** East side of The Forest: local bus (most lines) from Upper Parliament Street, near its junction with Milton Street; West side: tram from the city centre | **Hours** Open access; free | **Tip** The Forest is especially appealing on a cold winter's day and, after a brisk stroll, you can warm up at the very agreeable Homemade Café, beside the main walkway; for opening times, either call ahead or consult the website: +44 (0)115 978 1608, www.homemadecafe.com.

38 Gallows Hill

Eerie Victorian graveyard

Right up until the 1820s, the first thing visitors saw of Nottingham as they approached from the north was Gallows Hill, at the junction of what is today Mansfield Road and Forest Road East. Here, in full sight, stood the municipal gallows, a simple structure comprising two uprights and one transverse beam about four metres in height. The effect on the visitor can only be imagined, but there again Nottingham was a famously turbulent city, so the local magistrates had a point to make about the consequences of law-breaking – and there were literally scores of crimes for which you could be strung up.

Nottingham's condemned were marched up from prison on High Pavement (see ch. 44) and, when the gallows came into view, they were traditionally offered a last drink at the Nag's Head at the junction of Frogmore Street; the pub is now student accommodation, but the white and black-trimmed stone building survives. The last man to be executed here was William Wells, who was hanged for highway robbery in 1827; thereafter the city's magistrates seem to have had a rethink and the gallows were dismantled.

The site of the gallows is now the entrance to the Rock (or Church) Cemetery, the spookiest of graveyards whose several footpaths dip and weave their way through an evocatively rocky landscape planted with a sprinkling of Lebanese cedars. Opened in the 1850s, the cemetery is crowded with those memorials so beloved of the Victorians: angels stand guard over some graves, others are surmounted by a broken pillar garlanded with a laurel wreath – 'Victory in death' – and yet others are topped by a draped urn, the return of the body to ashes. Here also, near the entrance, is a distinctive Portland stone Cross of Sacrifice, the standard signifier of a Commonwealth War Cemetery; over one hundred servicemen from both World Wars are either buried or commemorated here.

Address Forest Road, Nottingham, NG1 4HT, www.nottinghamcity.gov.uk/cemeteries |
Getting there Local bus (most lines) up Mansfield Road from Upper Parliament Street –
a five-minute journey, or a 10-minute walk | **Hours** Daily Apr–Aug 9am–6pm, Sep–Mar
9am–3pm | **Tip** Rock Cemetery is adjacent to the Forest Recreation Ground (see ch. 37);
continue north along Mansfield Road and you will soon reach the Forest's eastern entrance.
There are occasional guided tours of the caves – or catacombs – that honeycomb the sandstone of the Rock Cemetery; for further details visit www.visit-nottinghamshire.co.uk/
whats-on, or contact Christine.Duckworth@nottinghamcity.gov.uk.

39 Gannets

Go on – nibble at the carrot cake

Gannets – more formally Gannets Daycafé & Bistrot – is the sort of café every town should have. It's located in the old market town of Newark-on-Trent, some 23 miles from Nottingham, and it occupies neat and trim Georgian premises on the main street, near both the Market Place and Newark Castle (see ch. 62). Cafés have a tendency to come and go, but Gannets, which was established as long ago as 1979, has become something of a local institution, attracting business folk, idlers and shoppers alike. The décor is bright and cheerful and the furniture functional. Gannets is very popular and at lunch times it can be difficult to find a seat, which can involve some jiggling around, but it's all very convivial, particularly as you have to order at the counter.

From the very beginning, Gannets has been a family-owned enterprise committed to providing delicious food, with the emphasis on locally sourced and organic ingredients. There's a breakfast menu to get the day going, with offerings such as wonderful scrambled eggs, then you're into the regular daytime menu, supplemented by a brigade of daily specials, listed on the blackboard. Both vegetarians and vegans are well catered for at Gannets, as are youngsters, with a separate children's menu. There's nothing pretentious about the menu either: you can plump for something very straightforward, such as a Jacket potato with tuna, or try something a little more exotic, such as the mushroom and hazelnut lasagne. The range of salads often steals the show, however.

Be sure to leave space for dessert: Gannets' carrot cake is probably the best west of the Himalayas, allegedly prepared to a unique and secret recipe. Gannets also does takeaway food, and has a somewhat quieter upstairs room – hence the bistrot in the name – to which you can retreat if the hustle and bustle is simply too much downstairs.

Address 35 Castle Gate, Newark, Nottinghamshire, NG24 1AZ, +44 (0)1636 702 066, www.gannetsinnewark.co.uk | Getting there Train to Newark Castle, then a five-minute walk; by car, it's a 50-minute drive from Nottingham to Newark via Southwell and the A 612. | Hours Daily 8.30am–4pm, Sat 8.30am–5pm | Tip As an alternative to Gannets, try the Modern British menu at a nearby restaurant, Taylor's (www.taylorsfd.co.uk).

40 George Africanus' Grave
Nottingham's first black entrepreneur

A man with a mission, the educationalist and community activist Lenford Alphonso Garrison (1943–2003) made it his life's work to research and catalogue the black presence in British history. It's largely down to his efforts that we know anything at all about George John Scipio Africanus (1763–1834), who lies buried in the graveyard beside St Mary's Church (see ch. 95) in Nottingham's Lace Market.

Born in Sierra Leone, Africanus was brought to England when he was about four years old by his wealthy 'owners', the Molineux family, who educated him and are thought to have employed him as a servant at their home in Wolverhampton. Later, in the 1780s, after serving an apprenticeship in a brass foundry, Africanus moved to Nottingham, and this was where he and his wife, a local woman by the name of Esther Shaw, established their own business – an early form of employment agency, recruiting domestic staff via a 'Register of Servants'. It's clear that the business was a success, as Africanus was able to buy several local properties in the 1820s. But, as was common at the time, he was afflicted by the untimely death of his offspring: all but one of his seven children died in infancy; his surviving daughter, Hannah, married a local clock and watch maker in this same St Mary's Church in 1825.

A lack of personal records – diaries and so forth – means that we cannot know what it was like being black in Georgian Nottingham, but perhaps it's the inconsistencies that are the most striking feature: at a time when Britain was so deeply involved in the brutalities of the slave trade, Africanus was making a good living, as were a handful of his black contemporaries. The tomb of Africanus was uncovered in 2003, and is now marked by a green memorial plaque. His badly-worn epitaph includes the lines: 'Oh cruel death that separated here / A loving father from his daughter dear'.

City of Nottingham

St Mary's Churchyard
burial place of
GEORGE AFRICANUS
(1763 - 1834)
Nottingham's first
black entrepreneur

Sponsored by Nottingham Evening Post

Address High Pavement, Nottingham, NG1 1HN | Getting there Local bus (most lines) or tram to the city centre, then a five-minute walk | Hours For St Mary's Church and graveyard, check www.stmarysnottingham.org | Tip From St Mary's, pop across the street for a coffee and a cake at the cosy, family-owned Hungry Pumpkin Café (www.hungrypumpkin.co.uk).

41 George Brough Birthplace

Super-duper motorbikes

Lawrence of Arabia is not a name readily associated with Nottingham, but T. E. Lawrence (1888–1935) loved motorbikes in general, and Brough motorbikes in particular – and these were made in Basford, Nottingham. It started with George Brough (1890–1970), a motorcycle racer turned manufacturer, whose Brough Superior motorcycles, designed and optimised for speed and acceleration, were simply the best in the world throughout the 1920s and 1930s. In total, just over 3,000 Brough Superior motorbikes of 19 models were produced and they were immaculately made with each bike assembled twice: the first time for the fitting of all the precision parts, the second – after disassembly for hand painting and plating – for the creation of the finished item. Production of these Brough Superior motorbikes began in the 1920s and continued until 1940, when the factory switched to war work.

These speedy motorbikes were ideal for Lawrence, who was to own seven Brough machines in all, with one on order when he died. Famously frustrated in his desire for Arab independence – the British and the French had shamelessly carved up the Middle East between them at the end of World War I – Lawrence had retreated to Dorset, where he took to tearing around the country lanes on his Brough Superior until – so the official story goes – he was killed when he swerved to avoid two boys on bicycles. The unofficial story is murkier: when Lawrence's bike was taken back to Brough, it's rumoured that workmen noticed the bike had car paint marks on it, indicating a collision with another vehicle. Accident or murder, no-one can be certain, but it is true that Lawrence's avowal of the Arab cause made him an inconvenience to the government. George Brough is remembered today by a plaque on the house where he was born, but his factory, on Haydn Road, has disappeared without trace.

Address 10 Mandalay Street, Basford, Nottingham, NG6 0BH | **Getting there** Tram to David Lane, then a 10-minute walk | **Hours** The house is a private residence, but you can view the exterior (and the commemorative plaque) at any time. | **Tip** The Victorian red-brick terrace housing of Basford spreads north and east from – and includes – Mandalay Street. There's nothing special to explore in the immediate vicinity, but you might venture over to Catchems Corner, a traditional boozer at 586 Vernon Road.

42 — Green's Windmill

Buy your flour here

Green's Windmill is a fully operational windmill perched on a hill in the Sneinton neighbourhood, on the eastern edge of the city centre. It was built in 1807 for the baker George Green Snr, who knew only too well the importance of bread to the locals. There had been food riots in the city just seven years earlier and, amidst rumours that bakers were hoarding supplies, his bakery was ransacked. This prompted George to write to the mayor asking for protection from the 'mischief being done to me'.

Green's mill was a financial success, as he had anticipated, but his son, also named George (1793–1841), who inherited the business, was a reluctant miller; he was much more interested in mathematics – indeed, his essays on electricity and magnetism were of seminal importance, though they never received the attention they deserved during his lifetime. After George Jnr, the mill continued making flour until it was superseded by steam power in the 1860s, and thereafter it was largely left derelict until its restoration in the 1980s.

Today, the windmill's brick tower, with its circular balcony, rises to a white cap, which is attached to its four sails, though at time of writing these are being refurbished. Inside, begin by climbing up to the fourth floor – the grain cleaner level – where you can inspect the mechanisms that make the whole thing work. The third floor – the bin floor – is where the grain is fed into hoppers, while the second floor houses the quartz millstones that grind the grain; the first floor is where the flour is sacked. Finally, on the ground floor, a flour-dressing machine separates the wholemeal flour into white flour, bran etc. Across from the windmill, there's a shop selling the mill's flour, as well as a child-friendly Science Museum with displays on the work of George Green Jnr. It's also a short stroll to the windmill's community garden, restored as a Victorian vegetable garden.

Address Windmill Lane, Sneinton, Nottingham, NG2 4QB, +44 (0)115 9156878, www.greensmill.org.uk | Getting there Local bus (most lines) or tram to the city centre, then a 20-minute walk; alternatively, take the bus from King Street in the city centre to Windmill Lane, from where a short, stepped footpath leads up to the windmill. | Hours Wed–Sun 10am–4pm | Tip If you've worked up a thirst clambering up and down the windmill, then pop over to the Bath Inn, on Handel Street, where a recent refurbishment has restored the Egyptian-style decorative touches that were added in the 1920s; it takes about 10 minutes to walk there.

43 Hardwick Hall

A magnificent Elizabethan mansion

Hardwick Hall is a stunningly beautiful country house some 24 miles north of Nottingham, just over the county border in Derbyshire. It owes its existence to Elizabeth, Countess of Shrewsbury (1527–1608), aka Bess of Hardwick, who rose to become one of the leading lights of Elizabethan England despite being born the daughter of a minor Derbyshire squire. Bess had a love of building, and Hardwick Hall, her major achievement, begun when she was 62, has survived in exquisite condition. At the time, the house was the epitome of fashionable taste, a balance of symmetry and ingenious detail, in which the crisp lines of the building are offset by a multiplicity of windows – there's actually more glass than stone – whilst up above, the countess's giant-sized initials (E. S.) intercept every roof line.

Inside, a special highlight is the top-floor High Great Chamber, where Bess received her most distinguished guests. It was here that she installed a fine plaster frieze that celebrated the goddess Diana, the virgin huntress – with the intention of pleasing the Virgin Queen herself. Next door, the Long Gallery is similarly gorgeous, from the splendid chimneypieces and tapestries through to a set of portraits, including one each of the queen and Bess. Bess and her friends could exercise here while keeping out of the sun – any hint of a tan was then considered distinctly plebeian.

Look out also for the hall's large collection of antique needlework, including several pieces by Mary, Queen of Scots, who was for years held in custody by the Earl of Shrewsbury. He moaned about the expense incessantly – one reason for the souring of his relationship with Bess, a deterioration that led to their estrangement. Outside, the garden makes for a pleasant wander and, beyond the ha-ha (the animal-excluding ditch and low wall), rare breeds of cattle and sheep graze the surrounding parkland.

Address Doe Lea, Chesterfield, Derbyshire, S 44 5QJ, but for Satnavs use S 44 5RW, +44 (0)1246 850430, www.nationaltrust.org.uk | Getting there By car, 24 miles north of Nottingham via the M 1, signposted from exit 29 | Hours Hall open daily mid-Feb–Oct 11am–3.30pm, Nov 11am–3pm; garden open daily mid-Feb–Oct 9am–6pm, Nov & Dec 9.30am–4pm | Tip It is perhaps a little confusing, but before Bess built Hardwick Hall, she lived in the adjacent Hardwick Old Hall, now a substantial if broken-down ruin operated by English Heritage (www.english-heritage.org.uk).

44 High Pavement

National Justice Museum at Shire Hall

Short, sweet and narrow, High Pavement is Nottingham's most beguiling street, its cobbles flanked by a charming ensemble of old buildings, mostly dating from the late 18th and 19th centuries. The architectural highlight here is the former Shire Hall, whose grand neo-classical façade – with its Ionic columns and bull's eye windows – dates from 1770, though it was poorly served by several modifications a century later. The main change was the addition of two doorways beneath triangular pediments just to the west of the entrance.

In Victorian times, Shire Hall was an all-in-one justice system with court rooms and two adjoining prisons – one for women, the other for men – plus a grand stone police station, which was added on the west side of the complex in 1905. It was here that justice – or at least rough justice – was dispensed, and it was also here, on a temporary scaffold at the front of the building in 1864, that the city witnessed its last public execution. The man concerned, one Richard Thomas Parker, had killed his mother and wounded his father; his demise proved a popular entertainment with a crowd of 10,000 turning up to watch his dispatch.

Shire Hall ceased functioning as a law court in 1991, and has since been converted into the National Justice Museum, which is mainly geared up for children. One high point of a visit is the Victorian court rooms, which remain in excellent condition, complete with seating and a central dock. While you're on High Pavement, be sure to take a peek at the basement-level doorway a few yards to the east of the Shire Hall entrance. The mason who worked on the doorway may have been skilled, but he clearly wasn't so hot at spelling: who he was no-one knows, but he carved 'goal' rather than 'gaol' on one of the external arches, then attempted to rectify his blunder – with the resulting correction still plain to see.

Address National Justice Museum, High Pavement, Nottingham, NG1 1HN, +44 (0)115 952 0555, www.nationaljusticemuseum.org.uk | Getting there Local bus (most lines) or tram to the city centre, then a five-minute walk | Hours Daily 10am–5pm | Tip Pop in for a drink at the Cock & Hoop, an attractively modernised old pub opposite Shire Hall, at 25 High Pavement (www.lacemarkethotel.co.uk).

45 Holme Pierrepont
Rowers ahoy

Well to the south-east of Nottingham's city centre, the River Trent worms its way past the flatlands of Holme Pierrepont, where the former gravel pits have been turned into a multitude of lakes with a variety of uses: some are kept as nature reserves, others are used for water sports. Archaeological remains indicate that the land hereabouts was first settled in prehistoric times, but the name of the place is a combination of the Norse – 'Holme' meaning low-lying land by a river – and 'Pierrepont', after the (French) lords of the manor, who arrived way back in the 1280s.

The village that once existed here is long gone, but Holme Pierrepont Hall has survived in fine fettle – a handsome red-brick structure, mostly two-storeys high and dating from the early 16th century. The house is still privately owned, by descendants of the Pierreponts, and stands next to the old village church of St Edmunds, whose somewhat ordinary exterior hides a handsome collection of Pierrepont family tombs; the finest is perhaps the alabaster effigy of Sir Henry, who died in 1499.

The Hall is on the edge of Holme Pierrepont Country Park, which occupies a large slab of land – and lake – on the south side of the River Trent. The choice of activity here is almost bewildering – from mini-golf and indoor cycling through to nature trails and climbing – but all things watery are top of the bill, most notably kayaking, canoeing, fishing and white-water adventures on a 700-metre stretch of (artificial) rapids.

The park is also home to the National Water Sports Centre, whose low and flat buildings flank an Olympic-standard rowers' racing course. Opened in 1971, the Water Sports Centre was largely funded by Nottinghamshire County Council at a time when they had both the cash and the vision. The Centre has had its difficulties since then, but still attracts top-ranking athletes.

Address Holme Pierrepont Country Park, Adbolton Lane, Holme Pierrepont, Nottinghamshire, NG12 2LU, +44 (0)115 982 1212, www.nwscnotts.com | **Getting there** Local bus 11C to the National Water Sports Centre, at the heart of the Country Park; 20 minutes by car; a network of well-signed lanes allows cars access to most, but not all, of the park. | **Hours** Park open daily 8am–6pm; activities usually need to be booked in advance via the website; Holme Pierrepont Hall is open only occasionally; see www.holmepierreponthall.com for current information on visiting | **Tip** Amongst the many outdoor activities on offer at Holme Pierrepont, one of the more unusual is *The Sky Trail*, which consists of a variety of nerve-jangling elements, including cargo nets, rope walkways and narrow beams. Navigate around them all to complete the course.

46 Home Ales Building

A striking Art Deco structure

Heading north out of Nottingham along the A 60, it's hard not to be surprised – even if you live here – by the imposing architectural charms of the old Home Ales office building, whose magnificent Art Deco clock tower rises high above its immediate surroundings. Both the tower and its adjoining wings are mostly of brick, soft brown with a hint of sandiness, their precise symmetries accentuated by a recessed attic storey clad in stone.

At the front, two rows of windows march along the wings, and between them is a cast-iron frieze depicting cherub-like figures enjoying a bit of brewing and carousing, all set against a pale-blue background. The tower once sported an illuminated sign boasting that it was the 'Home of the Best Ales', but – rather cheekily – the current owners, Nottinghamshire County Council, have replaced the 'Best Ales' part with their coat of arms. Look out for the main entrance, where an ornate, green-painted gate is set within a stone-clad frame.

Work commenced on the Home Ales building – and the long-lost brewery behind – in 1939, but this was interrupted by World War II, and the central tower wasn't finished until the early 1950s. The architect responsible was Thomas Cecil Howitt (1889–1968), who was about half-way along his professional journey from the Neo-Baroque Council House of the 1920s to the sleek Modernism of the Newton Building he designed three decades later (see ch. 67). As for Home Ales, the company opened its first brewery here in the 1870s, and blossomed as a family concern led by a series of Robinsons. Many of their brews carried names with a local theme – there was Robin Hood India Pale Ale and Little John Strong Ale – and their beer mats carried a Robin Hood logo too. Their brews proved popular, but not perhaps popular enough as Scottish & Newcastle Breweries gobbled them up in 1986, and that was pretty much that.

Address At the corner of Mansfield Road and Sir John Robinson Way, Nottingham, NG5 6DB | **Getting there** Bus 58 or 59 to Portland Street, then a four-minute walk; by car, the Home Ales office building is around four miles from the city centre | **Hours** Always visible, from outside only | **Tip** The 1937 Coronation Buildings, across the main road from the Home Ales building, is pleasant on the eye, and it's here you'll find the (wittily named) Abdication – an agreeable micropub with a cosy interior and a first-rate range of Real Ales.

47 Ibuprofen Plaque

A hangover cure – and much more

The driving force behind Boots (see ch. 16) for several decades was Jesse Boot (1850–1931), who was quick to realise that the working classes were moving from herbalism to patent medicines. As a result, he employed pharmacists to ensure the quality of his products before his main rivals. It was World War I that gave the company its major breakthrough, however: suddenly, a raft of medicines could no longer be imported from Germany, so Jesse assembled a team of experts to create their substitutes.

One result was an aspirin that Jesse heralded as the purest in the world. Another was a fast and effective water purifying tablet, which soon became a vital part of a soldier's kit. By the 1940s, Boots had established itself as one of the world's most innovative drug companies, with a well-funded research department established in the centre of Nottingham. Neither were Jesse's efforts entirely commercial: he and his wife, Florence (1863–1952), were determined to bring affordable healthcare to the average Briton.

In the 1950s, in laboratories on Nottingham's Pennyfoot Street, two of the company's leading scientists, Dr Stewart Adams and Dr John Nicholson, began experimenting with various drug compounds, the idea being to find a cure for rheumatoid arthritis. They didn't discover that, but in the early 1960s they did formulate a non-steroidal anti-inflammatory drug (NSAID) that greatly reduced pain of all kinds. It soon became clear that ibuprofen was safer and more effective than other pain relievers – and, as Adams confessed, perhaps tongue-in-cheek, it even tackled the effects of a bad hangover he was suffering.

In 2013, a Royal Society of Chemistry blue plaque was mounted at the site of the original laboratory, just outside the main entrance to BioCity's Innovation Building. Sadly, Boots, now part of a multinational conglomerate, no longer works on the discovery of new drugs.

ROYAL SOCIETY
OF CHEMISTRY

National Chemical Landmark

ibuprofen

In recognition of the pioneering research
work, here on Pennyfoot Street, by
Dr Stewart Adams and Dr John Nicholson
in the Research Department of Boots
which led to the discovery of
ibuprofen used by millions
worldwide for the relief
of pain.

21 November 2013

Address BioCity's Innovation Building, Pennyfoot Street, Nottingham, NG1 1GF | **Getting there** Local bus (most lines) or tram to the city centre, then a five-minute walk | **Hours** Open access; free | **Tip** Pennyfoot Street is set in the midst of what Nottingham asserts is its 'Creative Quarter' – an over-used description if ever there was one, though to be fair the modern buildings here are at least well designed.

48 Jamcafé

Funky European-style café-bar

With Goose Gate as its spine, the Hockley is Nottingham's liveliest district, its assorted bars, cafés and restaurants are busy during the week and heaving at the weekend. There's nothing prim and proper here – the city is much too boisterous for that – but the Hockley does have its own distinctive atmosphere, boho and relaxed most of the time, but mightily muddled at others, when it pulls in a very mixed crowd from the (very) dressed-down to the (very) dressed-up.

One of the Hockley's star turns is undoubtedly Jamcafé, whose attractive wooden façade, with its stained-glass windows and mini-pavement bar, is as welcoming as its interior, where an informal jingle jangle of fittings and furnishings is supplemented by a scattering of modern paintings. Bradley Rice, the sociable owner of the Jamcafé, took over the place about a decade ago, and nowadays one of his main focuses is on the drinks he serves. Natural Wines, vegan and produced with a minimum of chemicals, are the order of the day, as are craft beers with a rotating range of 10 keg lines and over 60 bottled beers and cans to choose from. One local brewery to look out for is Black Iris, which produces both the delicious Divine Elements (6%) and the tremendous Little Nipper (3.8%). You can also dabble in foreign beers. Belgium is well represented by three notable breweries: Oud Beersel, Cantillon and St Feuillien.

Bradley's other enthusiasm is music. Jamcafé mostly has jazz and blues as the soundtrack, but the owner also performs regular DJ sessions, with a propensity towards Afrobeat and Latin taking centre stage. There are also regular live performances, often featuring local bands of various genres. Most are relatively unknown, but Jamcafé has pulled in some big names, including the Sleaford Mods, whose abrasive punk-hop rants, voiced by Jason Williamson, rage against austerity Britain.

Address 12 Heathcoat Street, Nottingham, NG1 3AA, +44 (0)115 948 3566, www.jamcafe.co.uk | Getting there Local bus (most lines) or tram to the city centre, then a five-minute walk | Hours Tue–Thu 5–11pm, Fri 5pm–1am, Sat 3pm–1am | Tip Next door to the Jamcafé is Churchill House, a curious, cottage-like affair, whitewashed and set behind a miniature courtyard with an elaborate iron fence. Churchill House may have started out as the service wing to the more architecturally polished house next door, Morley House, currently empty but with a plaque inscribed 'The Peoples Hall, 1854'.

49 Junction Fish Bar

Dangerous criminal apprehended

Donald Neilson (1936–2011) was a career criminal, thought to have burgled over 400 houses before graduating to armed robbery. Nicknamed the 'Black Panther' for the speed with which he committed his crimes and for the black balaclava he wore, Neilson specialised in attacking village post offices, and he became the subject of a national manhunt after he murdered three of his victims in 1974. In January of the following year, Neilson diversified into kidnapping, when he broke into the home of Lesley Whittle, a teenage girl, whom he subsequently imprisoned in a drainage shaft. Neilson demanded £50,000 for Whittle's release, but the ransom arrangements were bungled, and the emaciated body of Neilson's victim was discovered in early March – much to the horror of the British public.

The police had few leads, and were it not for the sharp wit of two Nottinghamshire policemen – Tony White and Stuart Mackenzie – it's impossible to guess how many more people Neilson might have killed. When on routine patrol, the duo spotted Neilson acting suspiciously, and challenged him. Neilson promptly pulled out his sawn-off shotgun, told White to move into the back of the police Panda car, and forced Mackenzie to drive with the shotgun rammed into his ribs.

They soon reached the village of Rainworth, the location then and now of the Junction Fish Bar, beside the main crossroads. Mackenzie jerked the steering wheel from side to side, claiming he didn't know which way to go, at which point White took the opportunity to push the barrel of the gun away. Mackenzie hit the brakes and fell out of the car, but not before the gun had discharged, grazing White. These dramatic events alerted the unsuspecting queue outside the Fish Bar, some of whom assisted the officers, handcuffing Neilson and giving him something of a beating for good measure. Neilson died in prison.

Address Junction Fish Bar, 289 Southwell Road East, Rainworth, Mansfield, NG21 0BL, +44 (0)1623 491160, www.junctiontakeaway.co.uk | **Getting there** By car, it's a 30-minute drive north of Nottingham via the A60/A614 | **Hours** Mon–Sat 11am–10pm | **Tip** From Rainworth, it's just three miles south to Blidworth Woods, a slab of rolling woodland and heath that is very popular with local walkers.

50 Kaye's Walk

Two Luddites; one pistol

At 9.45pm, on 27 April, 1812, William Trentham was returning to his home at the corner of Kaye's Walk and St Mary's Gate. He knocked on his own door and, as he waited to be let in, two strangers emerged from St Mary's graveyard, just across from his house, and shot him through the chest with a pistol. Trentham's house has not survived and nothing marks the place where he was shot, but the narrow lane that is Kaye's Walk remains an atmospheric spot, with a graveyard on one side and old warehouses on the other.

As for the crime, Trentham survived, but the would-be assassins were never apprehended, even though this was no random act: Trentham was a hard-faced hosier, and his attackers were almost certainly 'Luddites' acting in support of the insurgency that had erupted in Nottingham the previous year. The Luddites were bent on securing more employment and better wages for the city's hosiery workers. Their main tactic was to smash the machines that threatened their livelihoods and the Luddite 'frame-breakers' raided factories in and around the city, always at night, and with covered faces to avoid identification.

Initially, the authorities panicked, especially when rumours suggested that the frame-breakers were being organised by an inspirational leader called Ned Ludd, or Captain Ludd. No such person seems to have existed, but when the Luddites wrote threatening letters to the authorities – as they did by the hundred – many were signed in his name. By 1812, the Luddites had refined their strategy, picking on hated figures – such as Trentham – and arguing their case in their 'Address to the Gentlemen Hosiers of the Town'. But the authorities were also on the move: Parliament made frame-breaking a capital offence, and extra troops were dispatched. These manoeuvres were partly successful, but improving economic conditions did more – and the Luddites simply faded away.

Address Kaye's Walk, The Lace Market, Nottingham, NG1 1PY | **Getting there** Local bus (most lines) or tram to the city centre, then a five-minute walk. Kaye's Walk is a pedestrianised lane running along the north side of St Mary's church. | **Hours** Always accessible | **Tip** To ponder the rights and wrongs of assassination, retire to the Kean's Head, an excellent pub at the end of Kaye's Walk; they serve a great range of Real Ales.

51 Lace Market Theatre

A charming little venue

Ambitious, progressive and ultra friendly, the Lace Market Theatre is Nottingham's most talented amateur dramatics society by a long stretch. Over the years, they have garnered rave reviews for many of their productions, which cover the theatrical gamut from Ibsen, Chekov, Rattigan and Coward through to more contemporary works like *Medea* by Euripides (via Ben Power) and Moira Buffini's *Handbagged*, examining the relationship between Queen Elizabeth II and Mrs Thatcher.

These plays are performed in a charming old building near the centre of the Lace Market that started life as a Georgian chapel, hence the fancy façade. Thereafter, it became a school, where William Booth (see ch. 108) of Salvation Army fame was a pupil, and then a paint store. Over the years, the volunteer members of the theatre have worked hard to keep their premises up to date, and now the auditorium, with its reddish chairs and proscenium stage, is comfortable and intimate in equal measure. On the floor above is the café with a serving hatch arrangement that is gently old fashioned, and a smaller stage, which is often used for art displays.

The Lace Market Theatre may be amateur, but it takes a professional approach to productions, with auditions for cast, and well-prepared 'Creative Teams' covering sound and light operation, wardrobe, set construction, etc. They also have open evenings where the theatre team and prospective members can get to know each other. It's twinned with two amateur German theatres, too.

The Lace Market Theatre's Christmas offerings can be one of the highlights of the calendar, eschewing the obvious in favour of a more inventive approach, sometimes with great success. 2022's Christmas 'spectacular' *The Flint Street Nativity*, saw adults play a bunch of scheming, double-dealing seven-year-olds, with a script written by Tim Firth of *Calendar Girls* fame.

Address 16 Halifax Place, Nottingham, NG1 1QN, www.lacemarkettheatre.co.uk | Getting there Local bus (most routes) or tram to the city centre, then a five-minute walk | Hours For performance times, visit the theatre's website | Tip Performances at the Lace Market Theatre usually end around 10pm – early enough to join the carousers in the neighbouring Lace Market on and around Broad Street.

52 Langar Hall

A fine hotel and restaurant in a country setting

When Imogen Skirving (1937–2016) inherited Langar Hall in the 1960s, she did not think she would stay long, but a dream prompted her to convert her home into a boutique hotel and restaurant, which she continued to run until her untimely death: she was hit and killed by a car whilst out walking in Menorca. Imogen was an unusual woman, Bohemian with more than a hint of spirituality, and she presided over her hotel with a gentle charm that attracted, amongst many others, fashion designer Paul Smith (see ch. 74), who stayed here regularly.

Langar Hall remains in the family today, and is little changed from her years here. As in Imogen's time, a long tree-lined drive leads visitors to the ochre-painted hall, a briskly elegant, two-storey, early 19th-century structure that sits in its own extensive grounds. Inside, the public rooms are a delight, a sort of antique pick and mix, from the rugs on the floor to the old chandeliers, and both modern and vintage paintings on the walls. The restaurant serves delicious food from a Modern British menu – try, for example, the pheasant with pancetta, swede and sloe berry – whilst the 13 guest rooms have all the bijou charm you might anticipate.

Next to Langar Hall is the church of St Andrew, an attractively proportioned, largely medieval structure with a square tower and battlemented roofs. The interior is a tad careworn, and rising damp is a problem, but in the south transept there are several finely-carved alabaster tombs, most notably those of the Scrope family. Curiously enough, the novelist Samuel Butler (1835–1902) spent his early years here as the rector's son. The family did not get on well – his parents were, the writer said, 'brutal and stupid by nature' – and Samuel's most famous novel, *The Way of All Flesh*, was a satirical attack on the sort of Victorian morality his father personified.

Address Langar Hall Hotel & Restaurant, Church Lane, Langar NG13 9HG,
+44 (0)1949 860 559, www.langarhall.com | **Getting there** By car, it's a 12-mile drive south-
east from Nottingham to Langar Hall via the A 52 | **Hours** Thu – Sat noon – 2.30pm &
6 – 8.30pm, Sun noon – 7.30pm | **Tip** It's something of a surprise to find that tiny Langar is
home to a sky diving company – Skydive Langar (www.skydivelangar.co.uk); prepare to dive.

53 Luisa's Vegan Chocolates
Sweet and delicious treats

Dating from the 1930s, the neat and trim, glass and red-tiled buildings of Nottingham's Sneinton Market have an attractive Art Deco appearance. They began life as the city's main fruit and vegetable market, but in the way of such things, the fresh produce market has moved out from the city centre, with more creative types moving into the old premises. Nowadays, Sneinton Market boasts a platoon of small, independent businesses, from a café and a cake maker through to a small brewery and plant shop. Together, they combine to generate an appealing, alternative vibe, and the market has become one of the trendiest parts of the city as a result.

Here, in the cosiest of premises at the heart of the market, is the outstanding Luisa's Vegan Chocolates. With flair and imagination, the owner, Luisa, and her daughter, Isabella, have developed a distinctive brand of vegan chocolates, which taste as good as they look – so good, in fact, that they have won a series of domestic awards for taste and quality. They sell a wide range of boxes of chocolate – for example Raspberry Hearts, Hazelnut Pralines and Peanut Butter Cups, not to mention ice cream in the summer. All of their products are made on site, and they are part of the 'Bean-to-Bar' movement, which involves actually making the chocolate, rather than manufacturing from brought-in, processed product.

Full marks for Luisa's ethical policies, too: she sources her cacao beans direct from farmers, and is well-known for paying rates above the market minimum. The beans she buys are top-quality, cultivated and then fermented in the correct way to bring out the full flavours. Furthermore, Luisa has visited Colombia to meet some of the female farmers she buys from. This was both to ensure ethical working conditions, and advise on cultivation in conjunction with experts from the University of Nottingham. A flourishing business, the future of Luisa's Vegan Chocolates looks distinctly rosy.

Address Sneinton Market, Unit 7, Nottingham, NG1 1DT,
www.luisasveganchocolates.co.uk | **Getting there** Local bus (most lines) or tram to the
city centre, then a five-minute walk | **Hours** Opening hours vary – see website for current
information | **Tip** From Luisa's, it's about 150m to one of the trendiest cafés in town: *Blend*,
Unit 30 (www.blendnottingham.co.uk), where the coffee is great and the food filling.

CRAFT CHOCOLATE

54 The Major Oak
Twang your longbow, Robin

The source of many a legend and myth, the Major Oak stands tall in a clearing in the middle of Sherwood Forest National Nature Reserve, on the edge of Edwinstowe, some 20 miles from Nottingham. No-one's sure quite how old the tree is – anywhere between 800 and 1,100 years at a guess – but it is indeed a mighty oak with a trunk circumference of no less than 36 feet, and a canopy spread of 92 feet.

Curiously enough, it was voted England's 'Tree of the Year' in 2014, presumably on the basis of the Robin Hood legends attached to it. One such tale has the famous outlaw and his Merry Men sheltering here for weeks on end, while another – and this is even more improbable – suggests it was here that Robin 'plighted his troth' to Maid Marian, either beside the tree or inside the tree: in fairness to the tale, it does have a main-trunk cavity just about large enough. It is, therefore, rather disappointing to know that the tree is actually named after a certain Major Hayman Rooke (1723–1806), a local antiquary who sang the praises of Sherwood Forest to anyone who would listen.

The Robin Hood legends may be fanciful, but they've certainly prompted the County Council to invest thousands of pounds keeping the tree alive. The chains attached to the Major Oak's crown were installed in 1908, whilst the supports propping up some of its biggest boughs arrived 70 years later, initially made of wood, but since replaced with metal. Until the 1970s, it was possible to walk right up to the tree – and even get inside it – but this was harming the roots, so now the tree is fenced off. This isn't too much of a disappointment, however, as Sherwood Forest holds several hundred ancient oaks, all unguarded, some bent and shattered, others gnarled and thick, but enchanting all the same, especially in spring when they bud; they are accessible on a network of clearly signed footpaths.

Address Sherwood Forest National Nature Reserve Visitor Centre, Forest Corner, Edwinstowe, Nottinghamshire, NG21 9RN, +44 (0)1623 677321, www.visitsherwood.co.uk | **Getting there** By car, it's a 20-mile drive from Nottingham to the Sherwood Forest Nature Reserve car park, then a five-minute walk to the Visitor Centre at the start of the Major Oak Trail (1.5 miles; 45 min). | **Hours** Visitor Centre open daily Mar−Oct 10am−5pm, Nov−Feb 10am−4.30pm | **Tip** From the Sherwood Forest National Nature Reserve, it's just five miles north to Thoresby, formerly a ducal estate whose salad days are recalled by Thoresby Hall (www.warnerleisurehotels.co.uk), a grand 19th-century mansion that has been turned into a hotel.

55 — The Malt Cross

A beautifully restored Victorian music hall

Right in the heart of the city, pedestrianised St James's Street may have seen better days – its assorted bars and shops look a little careworn today – but it does hold one real surprise. This is the Malt Cross, a pub-cum-performance venue whose heavily restored façade, complete with its slender columns, looks pretty much like it did when it was completed in 1877. There were once dozens of Victorian music halls up and down the country, but almost all of them were demolished decades ago, making the survival of Nottingham's Malt Cross really rather remarkable. And this wasn't due to its excellent management – a series of owners simply went bankrupt – nor the friendliness of the audience, who soon developed a reputation for boisterousness bordering on ferocity. Indeed, its reputation declined so much that its licence was temporarily suspended just before World War I.

But in 2014 the Heritage Lottery Fund funded a thorough restoration of the Malt Cross, and today the interior is quite simply charming. Slim cast-iron pillars with elaborate capitals rise from the wooden floor to support a balustraded upper-level gallery, which extends right around the place, with light filtering down from the glazed hoop-shaped roof; unusually, this roof is supported by laminated timber trusses (without nails or bolts), rather than the cast iron you might expect.

The current owners are an enterprising bunch, selling a wide variety of draft ales, offering a menu that's a cut above the bar-food average, and with modern art displayed on some of the walls, much of which is for sale. In addition, a pocket-sized stage hosts live bands, and there are all sorts of special events from 'Jazz Jams' to poetry readings and workshops. A separate entrance leads down to the sandstone caves beneath the building, once the place where the ale was stored, and now used as an extra performance space.

Address 16 St James's Street, Nottingham, NG1 6FG, +44 (0)115 941 1048, www.maltcross.co.uk | Getting there Local bus (most lines) or tram to city centre | Hours Mon, Wed–Sat 11am–11pm, Tue 11am–9pm & Sun 11am–6pm | Tip If the conversion of the Malt Cross from Victorian music hall to pub appeals, you might also like the Pitcher & Piano (see ch. 89), on High Pavement, though this time it's a church that's become a pub.

56 Meadow Lane

Notts County: the oldest football club?

Now languishing amongst the footballing minnows of League Two, Notts County Football Club lays claim to be the world's oldest professional football club, founded in 1862 – three years before Nottingham Forest. Nicknamed The Magpies, after the colour of the club strip, Notts County has played at Meadow Lane since 1910, and the ground, with a capacity of around 20,000, is a homely sort of place, with few of the fripperies that attach to wealthier clubs.

Of the stands, one is The Kop, from Spion Kop, a battle of the Boer War, while another is named after Jimmy Sirrel (1922–2008), a charismatic Scot who was County's most successful manager, in charge for three periods in the 1970s and 1980s; there's also a statue of Sirrel outside the ground, sitting on a bench with another Magpie hero, the trainer and general factotum, Jack Wheeler (1919–2009).

Notts County wasn't always a lowly club. They won the FA Cup back in 1894, and the sensational Tommy Lawton played for them from 1947 to 1952. In the 1980s and '90s, County even enjoyed time in the First Division – now the Premier League – but the club's recent history has been high farce. In 2009, a financial consortium bought the club and promised massive investment. Russell King, a convicted fraudster, was involved in the ensuing shenanigans, persuading former England manager Sven-Goran Eriksson, to become the director of football. In fact, it was all a sham – there was no money, and Eriksson departed a little poorer and perhaps a little wiser.

The next few years were awful for County. Managers came and went with alarming speed, but there was much mirth when, in 2019, County's owner accidentally posted a photo of his penis on twitter; inevitably, away supporters arrived at Meadow Lane carrying huge inflated penises. Things are calmer today, but County are still in a delicate situation.

Address Meadow Lane Stadium, Meadow Lane, Nottingham, NG2 3HJ, +44 (0)115 952 9000, www.nottscountyfc.co.uk | **Getting there** Bus to Meadow Lane; alternatively, a 20-minute walk from the city centre | **Hours** See website for details of regular guided tours | **Tip** Tickets to watch Nottingham Forest are hard, often impossible, to come by, not so at Notts County.

57 Mortimer's Hole

The tunnels of Nottingham Castle

Perched on top of a great chunk of crumbling sandstone, Nottingham Castle is the city's most evocative landmark. There's something for almost every type of visitor here, from an adventure playground for kids – Hood's Hideout – through to an excellent art gallery, well-tended grounds and displays on the city's history. What you won't get, however – and this can come as a surprise to first-time visitors – is a medieval fortress: the original castle was largely demolished in 1651, and today's incarnation, apart from a fortified gateway, is a grand ducal palace built on the orders of a local bigwig, the 1st Duke of Newcastle, a few decades later. It was his successor, the fourth duke, who brought trouble to his castle: the duke opposed electoral reform, whereas the local citizenry was in favour, so they set fire to his palace to teach him a lesson in the Reform Riots of 1831. It certainly put the duke off living here – and the castle was gifted to the city a few decades later.

The soft sandstone beneath the castle is riddled with ancient caves and tunnels. There are several entrances, but the longest tunnel is Mortimer's Hole, which winds its atmospheric way down from the top of the castle to the Brewhouse Yard below. On the way, you'll spy several mysterious side tunnels as well as a gun gallery, cut during the Civil War. Legend has it that in 1330 Edward III and his knights clambered up through the tunnel late one night to capture Isabella, the king's mother, and her lover, Roger Mortimer, who were planning to usurp him. In the event, Edward spared his mother, but things didn't work out well for Mortimer, who was hanged despite Isabella's entreaties: 'Fair son, have pity on gentle Mortimer.' As a boy, this author was enthralled by tales of knights in armour rushing hither and thither, and pestered his mother to come here time and again; my Mum, bless her, was very indulgent.

Address Lenton Road, Nottingham, NG1 6EL, +44 (0)115 876 1450, www.nottinghamcastle.org.uk | **Getting there** Local bus (most lines) or tram to the city centre, then a five-minute walk | **Hours** Daily 10am–5pm | **Tip** There are two cafés in the Castle – one near the entrance, the other in the Castle itself; the second is the better option both for the quality of the food and for the views over the city centre.

58 Murals at St Martin's

Beautiful murals, rediscovered and restored

Well-tended and well cared-for, St Martin's church – more precisely the church of St Martin of Tours – is tucked away amidst the Bilborough council estate, on the edge of Nottingham. Originally a small village church, most of what you see today dates from the 14th century, the trim exterior a study in contrasts, with the pinkish tones of the nave contrasting with the surly grey gritstone of the tower; there's a large modern extension, too.

Inside, the nave is neat and cosy – there's even underfloor heating – and all is in good order after a thorough renovation. What's more, the hooped wooden roof, added by the Victorians, provides a suitable frame for the most beautiful of murals, a gentle Primitivist work depicting the Annunciation. On the left-hand side, a kneeling, pastel-blue Virgin Mary, in perfect humility, has her hands in her lap, whilst a reddish archangel Gabriel, crouching on the right, has one hand raised as he announces that she will bear a son through a virgin birth. The murals were the work of Evelyn Gibbs (1905–1991), a talented printmaker and painter, who might not have come to Nottingham at all were it not for World War II: London's Goldsmiths College School of Art, where she lectured, was evacuated here and Gibbs came with it.

It's actually something of a miracle that the murals have survived at all. The Annunciation was one of several murals Gibbs completed in and around the city during the 1940s, but all were thought to have been lost over the course of the subsequent decades. Cue a merry band of electricians rewiring St Martin's who, in 2009, stumbled upon the top part of the murals above a false ceiling; it was a captivating discovery and the murals were restored thereafter. As for Gibbs herself, she remained in Nottingham after the war, and was a key figure in the Midland Group, whose aim was to foster the arts in her adopted home city.

Address St Martin's Road, Bilborough, Nottingham, NG8 3BH, +44 (0)115 929 8899, www.stmartinshiddentreasures.org.uk | Getting there Bus 77 to the Rose Inn, then a three-minute walk; by car, it's a 20-minute drive from central Nottingham | Hours Core hours Tue & Wed 10.30am–2.30pm, Sun 10.30am–noon | Tip Long ago, as dusk was falling, a tearful little boy was hunting for his lost pullover on King George V Park, not far from St Martin's. Yes, dear reader, that little boy was this author – so if you find his pullover (home-knitted and multi-coloured) please return it.

59 Museum of Timekeeping

Watches and clocks galore

The amiable hamlet of Upton, some 17 miles north-east of Nottingham, is distinguished by Upton Hall, a sprawling, bright-yellow country house built in the 1830s. The house has an attractive setting, in its own grounds, and, curiously enough, there's a grandiose entrance archway to the right of the main building that doesn't seem to lead anywhere in particular – no matter that it's decorated with casts of the Parthenon frieze.

Upton Hall was once owned by Albert Ball, the father of the World War I fighter ace Captain Albert Ball, who attended Nottingham High School (see ch. 110). Now, however, it's occupied by the British Horological Institute (BHI). Founded in 1858, the BHI is responsible for maintaining standards amongst the UK's watch and clock makers, and shares its premises with its offshoot, the Museum of Timekeeping, whose collection – the 'Timeless Collection' on its promotional leaflet – is both charming and informative.

The first room visitors encounter is the Grand Hall, top lit and equipped with a splendid staircase. Set against the walls are some of the museum's prime exhibits, including a number of antique long-case clocks and a lantern clock dating from the 1650s. Beyond, there's a room featuring several early speaking clocks, another devoted to the evolution of electric clocks, and a display on early time-keeping.

In the Watch Room, among much else, you'll spy Robert Scott's (partly rusted) pocket alarm watch. Scott's alarm was set to go off every two hours – the maximum time he could sleep before hypothermia threatened. Scott famously died getting back from the South Pole in 1912, so it's really rather amazing that his watch survived at all. In the same room, look out also for the super-reliable Admiralty Deck Watch, one of many such watches issued to naval officers in 1917, as an upgrade to the watches they had previously used.

Address Upton Hall, Main Street, Upton, Nottinghamshire, NG23 5TE, +44 (0)1636 817601, www.museumoftimekeeping.org.uk | Getting there By car, it's a 50-minute drive north-east from Nottingham | Hours Currently Apr–Oct Fri 11am–3pm, but may extend in future; check website | Tip From Upton, it's just three miles to tiny Hockerton, home to the sustainable, eco-houses of the Hockerton Housing Project and a first-rate gastropub, the Spread Eagle (+44 (0)1636 302208).

60 National Holocaust Centre

The Holocaust recalled and remembered

Laxton is an attractive little village, whose old red-brick agricultural buildings are an unlikely prelude to one of Nottinghamshire's most unusual attractions – the National Holocaust Centre – which occupies a wooded parcel of land just over a mile to the west. Quite how the centre came to be here is an interesting tale in itself.

In the 1980s, two brothers – James and Stephen Smith – went on a family trip to Israel. It was the first of several visits and, inspired by Yad Vashem, Israel's official memorial to the victims of the Holocaust, the brothers decided to create their own memorial back home. Their parents, Eddie and Marina, had long been running a non-denominational Christian conference centre in the Nottinghamshire countryside, so there was already some organisational history, but it was still a bold and adventurous move. The National Holocaust Centre they created was opened in 1995, since when its reputation has grown, and it now attracts school parties from far and wide.

A visit begins in the landscaped Memorial Gardens, a tranquil spot adorned with assorted art works as well as numerous name tags remembering some of those who died in World War II. Beyond, the original farmhouse is adjacent to a polygonal exhibition centre, a good-looking structure holding a first-rate display on the Holocaust, how it began and unfolded, with details of some of the individuals who perished.

One of the most striking exhibits is a display case holding individual items, such as a (forcibly-worn) Jewish arm band, and a handbag from one of those who was gassed. Naturally enough, the emphasis is on World War II, but there are also side features on, for example, the 'science' of eugenics, Jews in medieval England, and antisemitism in general. Everywhere, the text is succinct and clear, and the photographs simply outstanding – and often very moving.

Address Acre Edge Road, Laxton, NG22 0PA, +44 (0)1623 836627, www.holocaust.org.uk | Getting there By car, a 23-mile drive north from Nottingham via the A60/A614 | Hours Sun–Fri 10am–4.30pm | Tip From Laxton, it's just seven miles to the village of Caunton, where The Beck, on Newark Road, serves top-notch pub food – try the guinea fowl with parsnips, kale and pomegranate (www.thebeckatcaunton.co.uk).

61 National Ice Centre

Where Torvill and Dean first sliced through ice

Opened in 1939, Nottingham's first ice stadium was the arena where two of the most celebrated figure skaters (or ice dancers) of all time, Jayne Torvill and Christopher Dean, practised in their early days. They were both local people – Chris hailing from Calverton, and Jayne from Clifton – and in the 1970s they were brought together as a skating partnership by a prescient local coach, who spotted their talent and ambition.

Over the subsequent decades, Torvill and Dean won international competitions galore, before retiring from competitive skating in 1998. They are best known for their gold-winning performance of Ravel's Boléro at the Sarajevo Winter Olympics of 1984, which brought them worldwide fame. The duo received the highest ever ice dancing scores for a single programme and, indeed, the performance is regularly voted as one of the greatest sporting moments of all time.

Nottingham was always going to be keen to capitalise on its ice dancing stars, and one result was the construction of a new ice stadium in 2000. It's hard to be kind about this ugly modern structure, however, which really is something of a monstrosity. That said, the stadium's ice-skating facilities are second to none, with two large ice rinks: the first is part of the National Ice Centre, the second the adjoining Motorpoint Arena, though the names are effectively interchangeable.

The Motorpoint rink is home to the top-ranking Nottingham Panthers ice hockey team and is often boarded over for concerts and special events. The National Ice Centre rink, on the other hand, is open every day and offers all things icy, from a recreational skate through to lessons in ice, speed, figure and synchronised skating. At the entrance to the Ice Centre, behind glass frames, are two sets of costumes worn by Torvill and Dean, including the one from the Sarajevo Winter Olympics.

Address Bolero Square, off Belward Street, Nottingham, NG1 1LA, +44 (0)115 8533101, www.national-ice-centre.com | **Getting there** Local bus (most lines) or tram to the city centre, then a five-minute walk | **Hours** Daily 9am–11pm | **Tip** Behind the National Ice Centre arethe assorted cafés and boho shops of Sneinton Market. In turn, the market adjoins a large, open square that is overlooked by the well-equipped Victoria Leisure Centre, whose splendid Victorian clock tower dates back to the time when this was a municipal wash house and public baths.

62 Newark Castle
Peaches or plums

Lording it over the River Trent, the eye-catching ruins of Newark Castle look a little haggard, but this was once an important stronghold, built to guard one of the main routes between north and south. The first major fortifications were erected here in the 1130s at the behest of Alexander, the Bishop of Lincoln, who had an eye for comfort – so he installed a residential suite or two.

The result was certainly considered grand enough to accommodate kings and queens, including King John (1166–1216), who turned up here in October 1216. It wasn't a good week for John: he'd lost his baggage train in the murky waters of the Wash on the way, and once ensconced in the castle, he sickened and died. Rumours abounded as to exactly what happened: some accounts state that he ate a poisoned plum, others that he poisoned himself by eating too many peaches. No-one knows for sure.

Later, in the Civil War, the Royalists held the castle for the king, and the Parliamentarians made several unsuccessful efforts to winkle them out. The most determined assault began in late 1645 when two Parliamentary armies – one Scottish, the other English – invested the town. The Royalists soon began to starve, but held out until Charles I arrived and ordered them to pack it in – he had other, bigger fish to fry: Charles was about to surrender to the Scots, whom he hoped would prove more malleable than his English enemies; he was wrong.

After the Civil War, the castle was slighted and left derelict until the 1840s, when the ruins were brought to order and partially restored; the park-like public gardens beside the castle came a little later and will, in the next year or two, be landscaped and expanded. The best view of the castle is from the west (river) side. From this angle, the long curtain wall stretches along the river bank, intercepted by a series of towers; the imposing ashlar-fronted gatehouse is just visible at the north-east corner.

Address Castle Gate, Newark, Nottinghamshire, NG24 1BG | Getting there Train to Newark Castle, then a three-minute walk; by car, it's a 50-minute drive from Nottingham to Newark via Southwell and the A 612 | Hours Daily 9am–dusk | Tip If the castle stirs your interest in the Civil War, it's just a seven-minute walk to the National Civil War Centre & Museum (www.nationalcivilwarcentre.com).

63 New Art Exchange

Contemporary art gallery with a multicultural edge

Hyson Green, a mile or so north of the city centre, is a gritty, inner-city neighbourhood whose epicentre is usually reckoned to be the junction of Gregory Boulevard and Radford Road – and it's here you'll find the New Art Exchange (NAE), a contemporary art gallery with a community/multicultural mission. Thoughts on developing this type of art gallery here began in the early 2000s. This was partly at the instigation of Len Garrison (1943–2003), a historian and community activist who – with every justification – felt that British schools took scant notice of black history and culture.

As part of his endeavours, Garrison helped establish East Midlands African Caribbean Arts (EMACA) and worked on the life and times of one of Nottingham's early black entrepreneurs, George Africanus (see ch. 40). Finally, in the early 2000s, plans crystallised for the construction of a Hyson Green gallery, and architects Hawkins/Brown were brought in to design the building. The result is a handsome cubic structure, a block of black brick with a scattering of windows at different heights and of different sizes. Opened in 2008, the NAE incorporates one large and two small inter-connected galleries on the ground floor, a performance space and modest mezzanine gallery above.

Over the years, the NAE has organised a variety of temporary exhibitions, some obscure or avant-garde, others less so, that have helped raise the profile of many black and Asian artists. Inevitably, these exhibitions have ranged in quality, but the best – such as an audio-visual installation called Floating Coffins, and a trilogy of films by Hetain Patel – have garnered rave reviews. The NAE also takes its community brief seriously, organising all sorts of classes and workshops, many for children. They have, for example, recently fostered the work of WondHERland, a local all-female music collective.

Address 39–41 Gregory Boulevard, Nottingham, NG7 6BE, +44 (0)115 924 8630, www.nae.org.uk | Getting there Tram to Forest, then a short walk | Hours Tue–Sat 10am–4pm | Tip It's a couple of tram stops north from The Forest to the rather unusual Valve Shop, at 398 Radford Road. Tatty from the outside, the shop is literally rammed to the gunnels – electrical stuff via the door on the left, car stuff on the right. What's amazing is the staff: ask and they disappear to unearth almost anything you require. Electricians and mechanics love the place.

64 New Castle House
A fine Art Deco building

Lace may have been the apple of many a Nottingham merchant's eye, but it was just one aspect of a massive textile industry that flourished throughout the East Midlands, until its dramatic demise began in the 1970s. More than anything else, the local textile industry was massacred by foreign competition, but it was always a febrile business subject to the vagaries of both fashion and technological developments – and New Castle House illustrates the point to perfection.

The building was constructed back in the early 1930s for William Hollins & Company, one of the big names of the textile industry. A handsome, self-confident structure – despite some modern tinkering – the building's Art Deco façade, with its jaunty clock, features acres of glass set within a slender concrete frame. When it was built – as Viyella House – the company's future looked rosy. Back in the 1890s they had invented Viyella, a blend of merino wool and cotton that proved incredibly popular. Then, during World War I, they developed a related product, Clydella, which proved just as hot an item for men's shirts. After the war, however, things began to go awry. In 1961, the company was swallowed up into Viyella International by Joe Hayman (1921–1999), an aggressive tycoon who created a monster of a domestic textile company.

Hyman made a spirited attempt to increase sales by forging an association between Viyella and 'sex, romance and fast cars', but this evaporated after he was usurped in 1969. Hayman's business strategy was to prove illusory in other ways, too. He believed that Far Eastern textiles should be left to dominate the cheaper end of the market, whilst British companies stuck to higher-quality products – a pipe dream if ever there was one. Typically, New Castle House is now used for offices – with not a textile worker in sight, though at least it's now protected as a Grade II-listed building.

NEW CASTLE HOUSE

Address Castle House, Castle Boulevard, Nottingham, NG7 1FT | Getting there Local bus (most lines) or tram to the city centre, then a five-minute walk | Hours Visible from outside only | Tip From New Castle House, it's an enjoyable 10-minute walk to the precincts of the train station, where BeerHeadZ is an appealing if tiny real ale bar in the old cab man's shelter.

65 Newdigate House

Handsome townhouse and classy restaurant

During the War of the Spanish Succession (1701–1714), one of those interminable – and interminably bloody – wars that scarred Europe through the course of the 18th century, John Churchill, the Duke of Marlborough, won a famous victory over the French at the battle of Blenheim. One of the spoils was the French commander, Camille d'Hostun de la Baume, Duc de Tallard, who surrendered and was promptly taken to Marlborough: bodies may have littered the battlefield – over 27,000 French men were killed or wounded – but this sort of dynastic war was without aristocratic rancour. Consequently, when Marlborough met Tallard he declared 'I am very sorry that such a cruel misfortune should have fallen upon a soldier for whom I have the highest regard'.

But then there was the problem of what to do with such a prominent prisoner. In the event, Tallard was ushered into gentlemanly captivity, first with the Duke of Devonshire at his stately pile in Chatsworth, Derbyshire, and then in Nottingham, at Newdigate House, a capacious late 17th-century townhouse, whose exterior has survived in excellent condition. A handsome symmetrical structure of three storeys with 14 mullion windows, the house's brickwork is rendered in a muted cream, and the front door is positioned beneath a broken pediment that once held a carved bust.

Tallard was confined here at Newdigate House for six years, whiling away his time by creating a formal garden that was much admired by a string of visitors, including Daniel Defoe. Tallard is also credited with introducing celery to the English dining table, so it is singularly appropriate that Newdigate House – and its modern extension – are now home to one of the city's best restaurants, World Service, where the menu is Modern British: try, for example, the pork fillet with cauliflower, confit potatoes, apple and tarragon, or the loin of lamb with seaweed, asparagus tart and Jersey potatoes.

Address Newdigate House, Castle Gate, Nottingham, NG1 6AF, +44 (0)115 847 5587, www.worldservicerestaurant.com | Getting there Local bus (most lines) or tram to the city centre, then a five-minute walk | Hours Restaurant: reservation times Wed 6–9pm, Thu noon–2pm & 6–9pm, Fri & Sat noon–2pm & 6–9.30pm, Sun noon–3.30pm | Tip Across from Newdigate House, the other side of Castle Gate sports an especially harmonious ensemble of old town houses, including numbers 43–47, built for the lawyer Cornelius Launder in the 1780s.

66 Newstead Abbey Gardens

A beguiling must-see for garden lovers

The grounds and gardens of Newstead Abbey, some 11 miles north of Nottingham, are simply delightful. Starting at the dinky little gatehouse, beside the A 60, a narrow approach road threads its way past swathes of rhododendron bound for the abbey and its gardens – though 'abbey' is something of a misnomer, as it's now more of a country house (see ch. 23). The elongated front of the house is a tad graceless, but it's attached to the beautiful west façade of the former abbey church, dating from the late 13th century, and complete with the figure of a seated Mary and baby Jesus right at the top.

The house faces out over both the Upper Lake, which was once used for pocket-sized naval re-enactments, as per the aristocratic fashion of the time, and the former stables, a comely mid-Victorian complex with a prominent tower. At its southern end, the water from the Upper Lake cascades over a weir before gurgling its way down towards the Garden Lake. Just beyond this second lake is the lovely Japanese Garden, whose miniature bridges, rockeries, stepping stones and stone lanterns are criss-crossed by the narrowest and most charming of footpaths.

Tracking back towards the house from the Japanese Garden, past the Fernery, which was added in the 1860s, you soon reach the Rose Garden and the Small Walled Garden, the first of a series of formal gardens, which culminate in the Great Garden directly behind the house, entered, rather picturesquely, through a narrow tunnel. It's here you'll find the trim classical monument that Lord Byron erected to his beloved dog, Boatswain, in 1808. The monument is inscribed with a long tribute to the animal, but as so often with Byron, all is not quite what it seems: cocking a snoop at religion, he thought he had placed the monument on the spot where the abbey's high altar had stood; although he miscalculated, the intention was there.

Address Ravenshead, Nottinghamshire, NG15 9HJ, +44 (0)115 876 3100, www.newsteadabbey.org.uk | Getting there Regular buses from the city centre drop passengers at the gatehouse beside the A60, from where it's a 25-minute walk to the house; by car, it's an 11-mile drive from Nottingham to the Abbey | Hours Park, grounds and gardens daily 10am–5pm | Tip From Newstead Abbey, it's just three miles south to the pretty little village of Papplewick, where the Main Street is flanked by immaculately maintained cottages that culminate in the Georgian elegance of privately-owned Papplewick Hall.

67 Newton Building
It's the cladding that counts

Few would argue that Nottingham's most imposing modern edifice is the Newton Building, a mighty structure that soars high above its surroundings on the north side of the city centre. Clad in finely-worked Portland stone, the building's clean lines and precise symmetries culminate in a distinctive tower that's set at an angle from the street, and rises in tiers above a grand and glassy entrance. It seems something of a wonder that the building was commissioned here at all, given that Nottingham had, at least at the time, the look of a Victorian city. But commissioned it was in the early 1950s, seeing completion in 1958.

Perhaps even more remarkably, the original plan envisaged two such enormous blocks with a courtyard between them, but the city council had second thoughts, and decided to scale the plan down. As it is, the Newton Building would not have looked amiss in Stalin's Moscow and, for that matter, you can imagine Winston Smith working here for the Ministry of Truth in Orwell's *1984*. Yet, the overseeing architect was not some modernist hot shot, but Nottingham's own Thomas Cecil Howitt (1889–1968), one time city planner and a man whose architectural sojourn took him from the neo-Baroque fancies of the Council House in the 1920s (see ch. 31) to the Newton Building 30 years later.

The Newton was designed as the home of Nottingham Technical College, which subsequently morphed into Nottingham Trent Polytechnic and, in 1992, Nottingham Trent University. A glazed atrium at the back of the Newton Building now connects it with the contrasting Arkwright Building, a neo-Gothic structure that dates from the 1870s. The latter's interior suffered bomb damage in World War II, and doesn't look its best, but the rolling stone façade, with its pointed gables, turrets, dormers and hooped windows, is seen to good advantage from outside on Shakespeare Street.

Address Burton Street, Nottingham, NG1 4BN | Getting there Local bus (most lines) or tram to the city centre, then a five-minute walk | Hours The Newton Building is not usually open to the public, but you can wander into the glassed-over area located between the Newton and Arkwright buildings at any reasonable hour | Tip Across from the Newton Building, on Burton Street, stands the Guildhall, an imposing stone structure completed in the French Renaissance style in the 1880s. No longer in use, the building's future is currently open to debate.

68 Nottingham Contemporary

One of the UK's best contemporary art galleries

Opened in 2009 as a major boost to the region's cultural scene, the avant-garde Nottingham Contemporary Art Gallery occupies a squat and chunky, green- and gold-coloured modern structure on the edge of the Lace Market, the most historic part of the city. This award-winning building, designed by London's Caruso St John Architects, references the old warehouses of the Lace Market, but although the concrete façade is indeed embedded with a Victorian cherry blossom lace design, many locals find the cross referencing a little difficult to discern.

Inside, a large and capacious foyer holds a pleasant art-orientated book and gift shop, which serves as an agreeable prelude to four adjoining and inter-connected galleries. It's here that the Contemporary mounts half a dozen major exhibitions every year, covering a wide range of themes and subjects, some very challenging, others more populist / popular. One of the most successful was a large and ambitious exhibition entitled 'Kafou: Haiti, Art and Vodou', which tracked the remarkable history of Haiti's popular art over seven decades. A second success showcased the early works of David Hockney, whereas 'Aquatopia: The Imaginary of the Ocean Deep' – described as a 'transhistorical, transcultural voyage through the oceanic imaginary' – was of more specialist appeal. A stairway, framed by heavy concrete walls, leads down from this floor to the café, which comes complete with an attractive outside terrace, as well as a space set aside for performance, film showings and special events.

The Contemporary's founding director was Alex Farquharson, who garnered rave reviews for many of his exhibitions, enough to earn himself artistic promotion: he is now the director of Tate Britain. The current curator is Salma Tuqan.

Address Weekday Cross, Nottingham, NG1 2GB, +44 (0)115 948 9750, www.nottinghamcontemporary.org | Getting there Local bus (most lines) or tram to the city centre, then a five-minute walk | Hours Tue–Sat 10am–6pm, 11am–5pm; free entry | Tip A standard-issue street today, Weekday Cross, abutting Nottingham Contemporary, was once the site of an important market place, its more significant days recalled by the stone cross that was reinstated here in the 1990s. Incidentally, many of the streets around here are named 'gate' reflecting Nottingham's occupation by the Danes, who first captured the city in 868.

69 Nottingham Playhouse
Theatrical home of Anish Kapoor's Sky Mirror

In the early 1960s, there was a concerted effort to raise Nottingham's artistic profile. One result was the construction of Nottingham Playhouse, which was built in the full flush of the Modernist style to a design by the German-born architect Peter Moro. Locally, there were mixed feelings about the design – some admired the curved, concrete auditorium walls, others did not – but it was certainly adaptable: the Playhouse can adopt either a proscenium or thrust stage, offering great versatility.

The Playhouse got off to a cracking start under the artistic direction of Frank Dunlop and the illustrious John Neville, but by 1967 both had gone – Neville allegedly resigning over funding disputes with the Arts Council. Since then, Nottingham Playhouse has perhaps had more than its fair share of theatrical ups and downs, though its longstanding Christmas pantomime is reliably hilarious, and a major source of income.

The building has itself been subject to the vagaries of fortune: in the 1980s, the concrete interiors looked particularly ugly, and a clumsy refurbishment ensued, but a more recent upgrade has restored much of the structure's architectural integrity, and it's now a Grade II listed building.

The Playhouse's appearance has also greatly benefited from the conspicuous Sky Mirror, positioned on the pavement terrace just outside the entrance. Made in Finland and installed in 2001, this outstanding piece of street art was created by the sculptor and conceptual artist Anish Kapoor. It comprises a six-metre-wide concave dish of polished stainless steel, weighing 10 tonnes and angled up towards the sky. One local newspaper suggested that the mirror would 'fry pigeons to death', but the winged pests have been unaffected, with the Sky Mirror voted the city's favourite landmark on several occasions – despite the hefty wedge of money it cost to install.

Address Wellington Circus, Nottingham, NG1 5AF, +44 (0)115 941 9419, www.nottinghamplayhouse.co.uk | **Getting there** Local bus (most lines) or tram to the city centre, then a five-minute walk | **Hours** Sky Mirror: open access; free; call box office or check website for Playhouse performance times | **Tip** If you want to find your voice, consider joining the Nottingham Playhouse Choir: you don't need to be able to read music, just have a desire to participate and sing; further details available on the website.

70 Nottingham Station

Attractive Edwardian railway station

In the middle of the 19th century, there was a mad dash to connect almost every British town and village to the rail network. As part of this headlong rush, the railway reached Nottingham in 1839, when the Midland Counties Railway connected the city to Derby, which was, as one local wag put it, the worst possible option, reflecting the (generally tongue-in-cheek) rivalry between the two neighbours. Sixty years later and there were train lines heading out of Nottingham in all directions, with competing companies slugging it out.

The first major game changer was when two of these companies combined to build Victoria Station, a grand and massively expensive structure, which opened in the centre of Nottingham in 1900. Sadly, this was demolished in the late 1960s – with the exception of its heavy-duty clock tower, which now stands rather forlornly beside the Victoria Centre shopping mall. But its construction stirred the rival Midland Railway into action: in 1904, they opened a new station, originally Nottingham Midland, now simply Nottingham Station.

Benefitting from a recent upgrade, Nottingham Station is a handsome and inviting structure. It was built in a style that can only be described as Edwardian Neo-Baroque, its reddish-pink terracotta frontage surmounted by a domed clock tower and punctuated by elaborate carriage archways, which are set beneath garlands of fruit. In a clever stroke, the station is on a road bridge above the platforms, where, on Platform 5, amongst a ramble of good-looking little offices, you'll find a sweet little waiting room with stained-glass windows and a frieze of cherubs.

Curiously, the long-gone railway line from Victoria Station once overshot Nottingham Station – much to the chagrin of Midland Railway bosses – and you can still see the old line's approximate route as it now serves as the route for the city's trams.

Address Carrington Street, Nottingham, NG2 3AQ | **Getting there** Frequent trams to the railway station from the city centre, or walk in about ten minutes | **Hours** Open access; free | **Tip** If railway buildings are your thing, then proceed to London Road, just a five-minute walk from Nottingham Station, where the Great Northern Station (aka the London Road Station) is a good-looking structure built in the 1850s. This disused station, now a Virgin Active Health Club, is distinguished by its fine, stone-trimmed brickwork, long and slender chimneys and elegant covered entrance.

71 Ossington Coffee Palace
Newark's temperance hidey-hole

As you approach Newark from the west, it's near enough impossible to miss the Ossington Coffee Palace – a large, curious, if not positively eccentric building standing tall across the street from Newark Castle (see ch. 62). This is the town's finest Victorian building, though the architects, Ernest George & Peto – brought here from London at great expense – boasted that it was, in fact, a 'perfect model of a 17th-century hostelry'.

To achieve this vision, the architects opted for the then popular Old English style, with long and slender brick chimneys, oriel windows interspersed by plasterwork panels, ground-level bays, and a clutch of dormer windows. When it was completed in 1882, the Ossington had stables, a reading room, a billiard room, a library, dormitory accommodation for travellers, and a café with a terraced garden that stretched down to the river.

The cost of the whole project, from the purchase of the land to the construction, was met by an aristocrat with local connections, Charlotte, the Viscountess Ossington (1806 – 1889) – sister of the 'burrowing' 5th Duke of Portland over in Newstead Abbey (see ch. 23). In due course, Charlotte gifted the Ossington to the municipality of Newark, but this was no whimsical act of generosity: above all else, the Viscountess wanted to provide Newark with a Temperance house, a respectable hostelry where coffee was championed rather than the demon drink.

Unfortunately for Charlotte, many of the good citizens of Newark were not inclined to be saved from themselves, preferring the taverns of the town to the Ossington Palace, which soon flopped. It was sold off and turned into a private hotel the year of her death. Since then, the Ossington has had a bumpy history, including time as an (alcohol-serving) restaurant; it's now largely unoccupied, though a sensitive revamp may be in the offing.

Address Beastmarket Hill, Newark, Nottinghamshire, NG24 1BH | **Getting there** Train to Newark Castle, then a five-minute walk; by car, it's a 50-minute drive from Nottingham to Newark via Southwell and the A 612 | **Hours** Currently not open to the public | **Tip** Newark is an historic town and, if the weather is good, you might be tempted to stroll around the perimeter of its most unique attraction, the Queen's Sconce, the earthen fortifications raised during the Civil War siege of 1645/6; it takes about 20 minutes to get to the Sconce on foot from the Ossington.

72 Papplewick Pumping Station

The sandstone purifies the water

Gloriously Victorian, Papplewick Pumping Station, around nine miles north of Nottingham, looks more like a country estate than an industrial utility – from its ornate entrance gate and gate-lodge superintendent's house through to its well-tended gardens and decoratively-shaped pool. Yet the pool, on which model boats now zip around, is in fact the Cooling Pond for the machinery of the neighbouring Engine House, a sturdy, red-brick structure with a handful of architectural peccadilloes added to lighten its bulk.

Dating from the 1880s, the pumping station was built to meet Nottingham's burgeoning demand for fresh water – just 30 years or so after the link between water-born diseases such as cholera and typhoid and the water supply had been firmly established. Nottingham's chief engineer, the splendidly named Marriott Ogle Tarbotton (1834–1887), took control of affairs, determined to sink a well deep enough to tap the water lying in the sandstone. Today, visitors can inspect the results of Tarbotton's endeavours, beginning with the Boiler House, which is equipped with six large and immaculately maintained boilers, before moving on to the adjacent Engine House, home to two magnificent James Watt & Co. beam engines. It was here that Tarbotton excelled himself, adding all sorts of naturalistic decoration to the cast-iron columns – fish, cranes and water lilies for example – and even a set of stained-glass windows.

The best time to visit is on Steam Days, when the boilers are stoked and the beam engines swing into action. To the rear of the Boiler and Engine House is a group of service buildings, including a working blacksmith's forge and the coal store, as well as a remarkably tall chimney for the smoke from the Boiler House. Also, up the hill behind – and visitable on Steam Days – is the original subterranean reservoir.

Address Rigg Lane, Ravenshead, NG15 9AJ, +44 (0)115 963 2938, www.papplewickpumpingstation.org.uk | **Getting there** By car, a nine-mile drive north from Nottingham via the A 614 | **Hours** Non-Steaming Days Apr–Oct usually Wed & Sun 11am–3pm; Steaming Days are once or twice a month except in winter – see website for details. | **Tip** For fans of Victorian pumping stations, the similarly well-preserved, if not quite as grand, Bestwood Pumping Station is beside the A 60, just three miles south, but although you can usually wander around the place, it no longer caters to the general public.

73 __ Park Estate & Park Tunnel

The tunnel that never worked

Distinct and distinctive, the Park Estate holds many of Nottingham's finest Victorian mansions, its winding streets filling out a hilly slab of land to the immediate west of the city centre. This was once a forested deer park set aside for the castle garrison, but the land passed into private ownership when William Cavendish, the 1st Duke of Newcastle, bought both the (ruined) castle and the park in 1663. His successor, the fourth duke, began selling off plots of land within the park in the early 19th century, and by the 1890s the Park had become the wealthiest part of the city, its development overseen by that most energetic of architects, Thomas Chambers Hind (1813–1899).

Most of the Park's handsome Victorian houses survive today – around 300 of them – although many have been split up into apartments. There is some remarkably ugly modern stuff too, but the Park remains in private hands with a board of trustees – and gas street lighting throughout.

Hine was also responsible for the construction of the Park Tunnel, which drilled its way through the steep sandstone ridge on the east side of the Park. The tunnel was to be the main entrance to the Park, allowing horse-drawn carriages direct access to and from Derby Road, but it all went wrong. Finished in 1855, the tunnel turned out to have a gradient of 1-in-12, which was simply too steep for the carriage-pulling horses, which slipped and slid as they tried to pass through.

Other entrances to the Park were subsequently developed, and the tunnel was soon neglected, but it remains a real curiosity. At 125 metres (410ft) long, it only takes a few minutes to walk from one end to the other. There's a central open section, where the more energetic visitors can clamber up a steep stone stairway, which curls its way up to street level – and the Park's Newcastle Drive / Park Terrace entrance.

Address The Park Tunnel, 33 Derby Road, Nottingham, NG1 5AW | Getting there
Local bus (most lines) or tram to the city centre, then a 5- to 10-minute walk along Derby
Road; the entrance to the tunnel is hard to spot as there's no sign and a modern apartment
block shrouds the entrance; the path to the tunnel begins directly opposite *Tough Mary's
Bakehouse* (see ch. 100). | Hours Open access | Tip Devotees of Victorian domestic
architecture may want to explore more of the Park Estate. One enjoyable route that takes in
some of the highlights is to proceed from the Ropewalk on to Park Terrace, which sweeps
round to Standard Hill (see ch. 90), near the castle; allow about 20 minutes.

74 Paul Smith's First Shop

From bikes to stripes

Local lad made good, Paul Smith (born 1946) is one of the most successful fashion designers in Europe. His rise to fame is a tale well told, beginning with him leaving school at 15 to work in a Nottingham clothing warehouse. At that time, his real ambition was to be a professional cyclist, but unluckily – or perhaps luckily – his hopes of a sporting life came to an abrupt halt when a cycling accident landed him in hospital for almost six months.

During his period of convalescence, friends encouraged him to enter the world of art and fashion, and Smith switched tack, taking tailoring classes before working for a Savile Row tailor. An ambitious man, Smith was never going to be satisfied with working for someone else, and in 1970 he opened his first shop, at 6 Byard Lane, Nottingham. This tiny shop became *the*place to be seen by Nottingham's fashion-conscious youngsters, with Smith soon developing his signature style, the bright, multi-coloured stripes for which he remains famous. As Smith explained 'We made them with something called windings, where you take a piece of card and a selection of yarns in different colours, then wind the yarn around the card to build up a series of stripes. Colour is three-dimensional, and so by creating the stripes you can see the colours at their most vivid.'

Over the years, Smith has expanded both his product range and international reach, and now has outlets in over 70 countries, with flagship stores opening in London in 1976, Tokyo in 1984, and New York in 1987, to name just three. There was also a whole brigade of collaborations, ranging from bespoke cars to wine bottles. The Paul Smith company remains independent, and although the original Byard Lane premises closed in 2017, there's a large Paul Smith shop close by in Willougby House, a grand, five-storey, 18th-century townhouse, at 20 Low Pavement.

Address Original premises: 6 Byard Lane, Nottingham, NG1 2GJ; current premises: Willoughby House, 20 Low Pavement, Nottingham, NG1 7DL, www.paulsmith.com | **Getting there** Local bus (most lines) or tram to the city centre | **Hours** Willoughby House Mon–Sat 10am–6pm, Sun 11am–5pm | **Tip** Willoughby House is just one of several fine old houses on this side of Low Pavement – but the stand-out is the wildly Gothic façade of number 10 with its fancy, grey columns and intricate, sandy-brown decoration.

75 Peggy's Skylight

Simply the best jazz club for miles around

In a great central location on the edge of the Lace Market, Peggy's Skylight is without doubt the region's best jazz club – indeed many music lovers argue it's one of the top spots in the whole of the UK. Opened in 2018, it was the wish fulfilment of singer-songwriter Rachel Foster, and her piano-playing partner, Paul Deats. The duo always dreamt of a place where visitors would feel cosy, safe and 'transported' by the music – which is exactly what they have achieved.

The interior layout of Peggy's, in what was formerly a plant and garden centre, is broadly similar to that of Ronnie Scott's, the legendary London jazz club: for the most part, it's table seating, some tiered, although there are also a couple of smallish bar-stool sections – and from almost everywhere there is an excellent view of the stage. The acoustics are first rate, and as the reputation of Peggy's Skylight has waxed, so has the quality of the acts: recent concerts have featured the trumpeter Bryan Corbett, violinist Andy Aitchison, saxophonist Josh Kemp and the soulful, funk- and jazz-infused sounds of Michon Young. Neither are Rachel and Paul averse to the likes of blues, funk, soul and ska with, for instance, a recent appearance by Dom Pipkin & the Ikos, whose music is inspired by New Orleans – think a souped-up version of Dr John.

An added bonus here at Peggy's is the food. The fare on offer isn't your run-of-the-mill stuff, but an inviting menu inspired by Middle Eastern cuisine. Dishes include, for instance, slow-cooked Greek lamb with a hint of chilli in a tomato sauce, and chicken, almond and date tagine. If you want to rattle your tonsils, you could also nibble away at Peggy's Pickles, vegetables in a sweet and hot liquor. The proprietors take care with the ingredients too: they make their own bread using bio-diverse Lincolnshire wheat, and their halloumi cheese is produced by a small family business in Yorkshire.

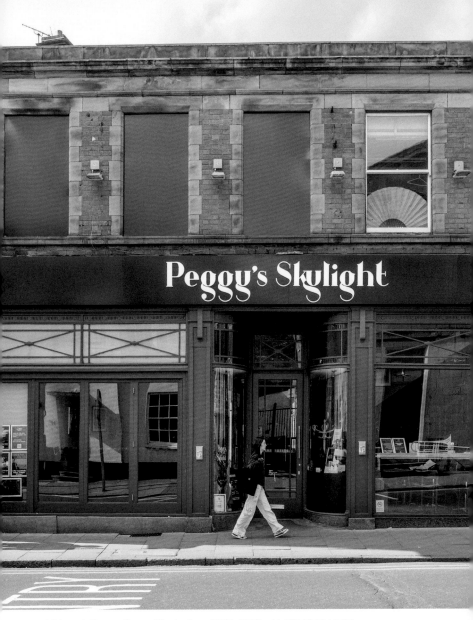

Address 3 George Street, Nottingham, NG1 3BH, +44 (0)115 924 0176, www.peggysskylight.co.uk | Getting there Local bus (most lines) or tram to the city centre, then a three-minute walk | Hours Variable hours – see website for details. | Tip Temperatures have been raised across Nottingham by threats to Peggy's future: the city council own the building and are thinking of putting it up for auction – but think of us first say the owners of Peggy's and their myriad supporters. Let's hope a solution is found.

76 Prudential Assurance

Perhaps Nottingham's finest Victorian building

The assorted businessmen who orchestrated Nottingham's booming economy in the late 19th century seem to have been more philanthropic than most and, indeed, some were determined to create a city centre to be proud of – with the pick of the buildings they left behind simply oozing municipal – or at least company – pride. One of the most striking – and one of this author's favourites – is the (former) Prudential Assurance Offices, a splendid even munificent 1880s edifice on a sloping, wedge-shaped plot of land at the junction of Queen Street and King Street.

Founded in 1848, the Prudential pioneered the sale of inexpensive insurance policies to the working class. It was a lucrative business, and in the 1870s the company decided to reinforce its commercial position by building prestigious offices in a string of provincial towns. There was nothing shy and retiring about their plans, so they chose Alfred Waterhouse (1830–1905) to implement them. Waterhouse was a dedicated exponent of the Victorian Gothic Revival style, and the man responsible for both Manchester's Town Hall and London's Natural History Museum.

In building Nottingham's Prudential, Waterhouse opted for a tapered and polished grey-granite base, upon which he constructed a pirouetting edifice whose several floors he decorated with an abundance of red brick and terracotta panels. At the top, he added a pair of Flemish-style towers, whilst the fancy entrance down below was framed by a dinky little statue of 'Prudence' – an attribute the company claimed in abundance. The Prudential moved out long ago, since when the building has had several owners, and the ground floor currently houses The Alchemist bar. Consequently, the interior has taken something of a mauling, but there remain hints of its former splendour, including some faience tiles and an original fireplace.

77__ The Queen's Chambers

Victorian flamboyance on the Market Square

Nottingham's Market Square – sometimes called Slab Square – is a wide and airy piazza that has long served as the social and commercial centre of the city. For the architectural purist, many of the buildings that flank the square are really rather undistinguished – and several have been poorly used in recent years – but taken as a group they have a certain stately charm and one of them, the Queen's Chambers, is a delight.

The man who was largely responsible for the design was Watson Fothergill (1841–1928), that most industrious of architects, who was then approaching the end of his career, having already peppered the city with his flamboyant constructions, mostly in the Gothic Revival style. Footing the bill in this case was a successful wine merchant by the name of Edward Skipwith. Skipwith wanted shops on the ground floor of the new building with offices and work rooms up above. After a lot of pondering, Fothergill went for a daring design in which the ground floor of the front elevation – facing out on to the Market Square – was opened up by a trio of freestanding granite piers. In turn, one of these supports a curious side-tower, equipped with gargoyles, a tiled and tapered spire, and alternating bands of coloured brick, whilst the bulk of the front façade has more bands of coloured brick, bay windows and terracotta panels.

Finally, this exercise, in what is often referred to as the Tudor-bethan Gothic style, culminates above in a half-timbered top floor, which makes the whole edifice look really rather jaunty. These stylistic features are repeated on the side façade, which stretches out along King Street, with the addition of a whopping chimney and a heavy-duty, red-brick tower-turret. Beneath the chimney is a small carved head of Queen Victoria, a surprisingly inconsequential piece considering the building was named to commemorate the queen's 60th Jubilee.

Address Queen's Chambers, corner of Long Row and King Street, Nottingham, NG1 2AS |
Getting there Local bus (most lines) or tram to the city centre | **Hours** Visible from outside
only | **Tip** There is a clutch of Watson Fothergill buildings in the city centre, but probably
the finest are a bank (see ch. 97) and his old offices (see ch. 104).

78 Radcliffe Road
The world's first tarmac road

Born in Swansea, Edgar Purnell Hooley (1860–1942) was an imaginative soul who stumbled across a combination of substances that quite simply transformed road transport – and it happened here in Nottinghamshire. In 1889, Hooley was appointed county surveyor of Nottinghamshire County Council. At the time, the 'county surveyor' was a brand new type of civil servant, whose purpose was to bring a sense of order to the country's chaotic infrastructure.

Hooley travelled the length and breadth of Nottinghamshire dispensing instructions and advice. During his travels – so one story goes – he noticed something very interesting as he passed a local tar works. A barrel of tar had been spilled on the road and, in an effort to clear it up, a worker had dumped gravel on top, thereby – entirely accidentally – creating a dust-free slice of road. Hooley was so impressed that he began experimenting with the ingredients, thereby inventing 'tarmacadam', a road surfacing material of heated tar, sand and crushed stone that he patented in 1902. Another version of the story gives even more credit to Hooley, claiming he spotted some natural tar when out walking in Derbyshire, and decided to mix it with crushed rock. You choose which one you think most likely.

Hooley may have been imaginative, but he wasn't much of a businessman, and found it difficult to sell his 'tarmacadam'. There were shrewder folk around, though, and one of them, Alfred Hickman, bought and relaunched Hooley's company in 1905. The Hooleys did not, however, disappear from Nottingham, running one of the city's largest garages and car sales companies for many years. As for Hooley's invention, the first stretch of 'tarmacadam' road was laid here in Nottinghamshire on the Radcliffe Road in 1902 – though, perhaps disappointingly, this stretch of road is indistinguishable from any other.

Address Radcliffe Road, West Bridgford, Nottinghamshire, NG2 5HG | Getting there Bus to Trent Bridge, a few yards from the start of Radcliffe Road | Hours Open access | Tip Let's be honest, looking at the first tarmac road in the world is unlikely to be gripping, but Radcliffe Road does start beside Trent Bridge, home of the Cricket Ground and from here it's just a five-minute walk to an excellent pub, the Stratford Haven (www.castlerockbrewery.co.uk).

79 Radford Boulevard Clock

All that remains of Player's cigarette factory

Nottingham made and manufactured, Player's Navy Cut cigarettes once ruled the waves. Unfiltered and strong, they were much prized by servicemen during both World Wars, at least partly because of the picture of the sailor on the pack with 'Hero' emblazoned on his hat band. At the company's peak, in the 1930s, Player's sold over three million cigarettes a year, employing several thousand workers in a maze of offices and factories to the north-west of the city centre on and around Radford Boulevard.

By and large, Player's – formally John Player & Sons – was a benevolent employer. Each worker had, for example, a free cigarette allowance (a mixed blessing, of course) and the company had its own sports grounds nearby on Aspley Lane, where this author made a singularly insignificant contribution playing for Player's Joiners football team. A job with Player's seemed as safe as houses, but in fact the company's position was becoming increasingly hazardous during the 1960s, as the link between smoking and cancer became undeniable. It's true that Player's was buttressed by being part of a multinational corporation – founded as a family concern by the first John Player (1839–1884), it had ceased to be independent in 1901 – but its days were numbered.

Player's tried to stave off collapse, building the new (and now demolished) Horizon factory on the outskirts of the city in the 1970s, but the launch of a new, non-tobacco/herbal cigarette proved calamitous – it was just such a disgusting smoke. In due course, Player's abandoned their showcase factories on Radford Boulevard, and these were then demolished to be replaced by today's retail park. It's here you'll find the Art Deco clock that is the solitary reminder of these grand factories; it was once attached to the main façade, but now perches on top of a brick column, in what has become a very dishevelled neighbourhood.

Address Castle Retail Park, Radford Boulevard, Nottingham, NG7 5QJ | **Getting there** Bus to Hartley Road, then a five-minute walk to the Castle Retail Park | **Hours** Always visible | **Tip** It's slim pickings here in Radford if you're after seeing anything to do with John Player, but the former Castle Cavendish Works, at the junction of Norton Street and Dorking Road, is a trim Victorian building with fancy roof ventilators that was once used by the company.

80 Ratcliffe on Soar

A power station and a village church

Like giant vases, the mighty cooling towers of the Ratcliffe on Soar power station, 10 miles south-west of Nottingham, have all the self-confidence of the 1960s, their tapering beauty – for in this author's opinion they are indeed beautiful – indicative of a time when coal-powered energy seemed the route to a prosperous future. They also reflect an era when UK power generation was a nationalised utility; in an eminently efficient arrangement, the Central Electricity Generating Board commissioned the power station and British Rail brought the coal – mountains of the stuff – from the collieries of Nottinghamshire.

In the coming decades, however, the gloss would come off coal-powered energy, as its damaging effects became all too clear. And although efforts were made to mitigate some of these effects here at Ratcliffe, it was all to no avail: coal-powered energy in the UK is doomed, with Ratcliffe on Soar power station scheduled for demolition in 2024, although many anticipate it will take a few years longer.

The power station takes its name from the neighbouring village, located just across the main road, and here, in striking contrast, a string of amiable, low-slung, red-brick cottages run roughly parallel to a loop of the River Soar. The village highlight is Holy Trinity church, a trim medieval affair with a spikey spire and a graveyard that is partly embanked to protect against river flooding. The church interior is fairly routine, but it's distinguished by a platoon of finely worked alabaster tombs dotted round the chancel. Perhaps the finest is the double-decker tomb chest on the right-hand side, where a chubby-looking Henry Sacheverell (died 1625) is laid out in his Jacobean armour, his three daintily carved children below and his three wives, shown in their long gowns and fancy headgear, kneeling in prayer up above.

Address Holy Trinity church, Main Street, off Kegworth Road, Ratcliffe on Soar, Nottinghamshire, NG11 0EA, www.453churches.com | **Getting there** By car, it's a 10-mile drive south-west from central Nottingham to Ratcliffe on Soar | **Hours** Holy Trinity is open daily 9am–4pm; power station not open to the public | **Tip** Motorists whizz past Ratcliffe on Soar on their way to East Midlands Airport, where one of the problems has always been its name: various options have been tried over the years, but Leicester, Nottingham and Derby have all had a hand in the airport, so none of them wants to give way to the other – hence 'East Midlands', though surveys show that only a fraction of non-Brits have any idea where the East Midlands actually is.

81 Robin Hood Bronze
Statue of Nottingham's legendary hero

In more modest times, in the 1940s, Nottingham celebrated its myriad connections with Robin Hood by commissioning a bronze statue of the medieval outlaw. Legend has it that Robin and his band of Merry Men hung out in Sherwood Forest, a vast royal woodland of oak, birch and bracken covering all of northern Nottinghamshire – and it was here that he (supposedly) robbed the rich and gave to the poor. Appropriately, the folkloric statue of Robin is located just below the fortified gateway to Nottingham Castle, which was, of course, the home and lair of Hood's bitter enemy, the Sheriff of Nottingham – though the medieval fortress is long gone, replaced by an imposing ducal palace at the behest of the Dukes of Newcastle in the 1670s.

The statue shows a youthful Robin drawing his longbow, for centuries the favourite weapon of the English, while plaques showing scenes from Robin's life and times are tiled into the wall behind. These tall tales range from the preposterous – King Richard I joining Robin and Maid Marian together in marital vows – to the apocryphal, with Robin and Little John fighting with wooden staffs as they compete to cross a timber bridge. There's also a really rather poignant scene of Robin firing his last arrow from his death bed: the story goes that the outlaw asked to be buried where it landed. In reality, although there's no 'true story' of Robin's life, it's the various legends relating to his death that are perhaps the most engaging; one version involves a treacherous prioress, who weakens Robin by excessive bleeding before the dastardly Red Roger of Doncaster polishes him off with a dagger.

Robin's statue is very popular amongst local folk, and has become the symbol of the city, though that didn't stop miscreants stealing his arrow again and again – until it was welded into position, solving the problem once and for all.

Address Castle Road, Nottingham, NG1 6AA | **Getting there** Local bus (most lines) or tram to the city centre, then a five-minute walk | **Hours** Open access; free | **Tip** Within ear shot of Robin is Maid Marian Way, the inner ring road, once christened 'the ugliest street in Europe'. Completed in the1960s, many hated the boulevard for ploughing through the oldest part of the city, others for its ugly modern tower blocks, but humour saved the day: watching pedestrians scale the barrier between the lanes became something of a sport, especially after alcohol had been taken.

82 Rock City

Brilliant night club with great live acts

Large and illustrious, Rock City has welcomed the city's youth for several decades, and its legendary student nights heave – literally – with undergraduates from the city's two universities: there are now over 40,000 students in Nottingham during term time, and a fair number of them are unable to resist the student night special – two-for-one drinks. Rock City's exterior is – for no obvious reason – painted an ugly shade of grey-black, but there's just enough detailing left to indicate the building's Victorian origins as a skating rink. In the late 1970s came its reinvention as The Heart of the Midlands nightclub, which hosted the inaugural World Professional Darts Championship, but it was all change again in 1980, when the newly dubbed Rock City opened with The Undertones, who finished off their set with the riotous 'Teenage Kicks'.

Rock City has been going strong ever since, the key to its longevity being its musical adaptability: in the 1980s, the club showcased the great rock acts of the day, but as early as 1982 it offered a Futurist night for techno-pop fans. Later evolutions included jazz, funk and soul nights, break-dancing afternoons and the hosting of Public Enemy for their first performance in the UK in 1987. In the 1990s came Punk, Grunge and Britpop – Nirvana appeared at Rock City in 1991 and Oasis in 1994. Musical events of note continue, with 2023 kicking off with Rock City's involvement in 'Beat the Streets', with multiple bands joining together to raise money for, and campaign against, homelessness.

Today, Rock City offers an outstanding mix of gig and club nights. The big-name artists appear in the Main Hall, with a capacity for around 2,000, and there are also two smaller performance spaces: the dark and somewhat mysterious Black Cherry Lounge, and Beta, an intimate venue that is especially good for catching up-and-coming bands.

Address 8 Talbot Street, Nottingham, NG1 5GG, www.rock-city.co.uk | Getting there Local bus (most lines) or tram to the city centre, then a five-minute walk | Hours Wed–Sat 10pm–3am; for information on events, check the Rock City website | Tip For a pre-gig drink, aim for Canning Circus, where there are two good pubs – The Falcon Inn and the larger Sir John Borlase Warren – both only a five-minute walk from Rock City – down hill too.

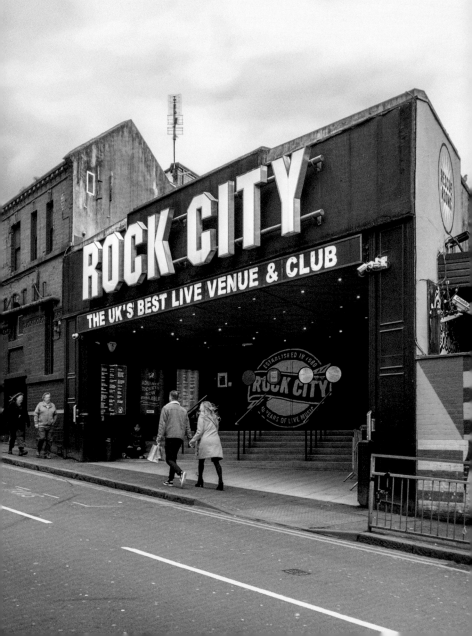

83 Rough Trade

Hurry here for the vinyl

It was something of a coup for the city when, in 2014, Rough Trade decided to open one of its shops here. There are few more illustrious names on the music scene than Rough Trade, and Stephen Godfroy, the current director and co-owner, tipped his hat to Nottingham's 'esteemed independent music retail history' as one reason why he opened a store here – there are only five in the whole of the UK.

For a little historical context, Rough Trade began in the 1970s as a record store, which soon spawned an influential record label that signed some of the key music groups of the period – including The Smiths and Scritti Politti. These musical salad days did not last long, however, and the company's subsequent history has been complex, if not positively byzantine. Nonetheless, in 2007, Rough Trade took the bold step of opening a record shop in London. Many predicted failure – this was a time when the iPod seemed all powerful and record stores were closing all over the UK – but Godfroy's hunch was right: there was indeed a market for vinyl records in, as he put it, 'an environment where people want to spend time'.

Nottingham's Rough Trade shop follows the same formula. There's nothing formal about the place – if anything, the décor is really rather careworn – but customers browse happily on the ground floor, which holds an outstanding selection of vinyl, ranging from James Galway to The Clash, with jazz a particular forte. There's also a fascinating range of books: some of these, such as *Graphic Marxism*, hark back to Rough Trade's radical roots, while others focus on rock stars and cultural figures from Patti Smith and Angela Davis through to Lily Allen. Upstairs, a performance area offers an exciting programme of live music and events, from solo artists chirruping away through to 'Gladrags', an LGBTQ+ night 'celebrating drag, music and fashion'.

Address 5 Broad Street, Nottingham, NG1 3AJ, +44 (0)115 896 4012, www.roughtrade.com | Getting there Local bus (most lines) or tram to the city centre | Hours Mon–Sat 10am–7pm, Sun 11am–5pm | Tip Just off Broad Street, on High Cross Street, the distinctive rendered façade of Clumber Hall marks the last city-centre redoubt of the Plymouth Brethren, who hung on here for decades before the congregation finally faded away in the 2000s.

84 Rufford Abbey Park

A ruined country house and a walk in the woods

There was a time when Rufford Abbey, some 18 miles north of Nottingham, was really rather genteel, with its bijou jewellery makers and sculpture walk, but things are more popular and populist today – there's a crazy golf course, a large adventure playground and an archery range. On summer weekends and bank holidays, Rufford Abbey heaves, but at other times things are more relaxing, and there's still much to enjoy.

Precious little remains of the Cistercian abbey established here in the 12th century, but the Savile family, who came to own the place, built a grand house in the 17th century, then remodelled it in the 1830s. The remodelling was initiated by the well-connected 8th Earl of Scarborough (1788–1856), after whose death the property passed to Augustus Lumley-Savile (1829–1887), a society figure well known for both his skills as a ballroom dancer, and the fancy house parties he threw here – this was Rufford's heyday.

The substantial ruins of the house, complete with high gables and a slender turret, hint at past splendours, and the old main entrance is suitably dignified, comprising a two-storey porch framed by twisted (Salomonic) columns and approached across a dinky little footbridge. The house is the centrepiece of the country park, and behind is a well-preserved stable block with gift and fast-food shops. Beyond is an unusual bath summerhouse dating from the 1720s, semi-formal gardens, and the Reg Hookway Arboretum, planted with oak and birch and named after a one-time director of the Countryside Commission.

To the west and north of the house, footpaths thread their way through thick woodland and encircle the shallow waters of Rufford Lake. The lake's northern periphery is marked by Rufford Mill, a sturdy brick building that was constructed as a corn mill in the 1750s, but enlarged and converted into a sawmill a century later.

Address Ollerton, NG22 9DF, +44 (0)1623 677688, www.ruffordabbey.co.uk | **Getting there** By car, it's an 18-mile drive north from Nottingham to Rufford Abbey Country Park via the A60/A614 | **Hours** Daily dawn–dusk | **Tip** Curiously enough, 'car fishing' has become something of a big deal hereabouts, with spectators watching as motorists try to drive through the waters of the Rufford Mill Ford – mostly they make it, but sometimes they don't. To get to the ford (and try your luck?), turn off the A614 at the sign for Wellow, just north of the entrance to Rufford Abbey.

85 _ Shipstone's Star Brewery

A long-gone pint of best bitter

Though memories of Shipstone's have receded, this was once the dominant brewery hereabouts, with a pint of their bitter – always known as 'Shippo's' – marking the end of innumerable working days. Nottingham has been known for beer brewing since medieval times – its myriad caves were ideal for fermentation and storage – but it was James Shipstone (1820–1897) who brought a system to it all.

In 1852, this ambitious man opened his Star Brewery in Basford, and here he streamlined production, regularised his supply chain from top to bottom, and accelerated delivery to his customers. By the time of his death, his brewery occupied a seven-acre site incorporating maltings, brew houses, fermenting rooms and coopers' yards. Neither did he neglect PR: a red illuminated star at the top of the brewery's tower could be seen for miles around, and his drays crisscrossed the city, pulled by the most magnificent horses. In due course, the company was passed down through the family and the future looked good, but Shipstone's was more vulnerable than it appeared, and during the merger mania of the late 1970s, it was purchased by one of its rivals.

As part of a larger business, Shipstone's staggered on for another decade or so, but the boom times were gone, and the Star Brewery closed in 1991. There was then the problem of what to do with this massive complex. Fortunately, plans to have the whole lot demolished were rebuffed, and today, recycled for a variety of uses, it stands as a tribute to what was once a flourishing business, its imposing main tower decorated with a star-shaped clock and inscribed with the company's name. It's the tower and its adjoining red-brick structures that grab the attention, but a set of ancillary buildings stretching out along Radford Road are both interesting and strange to behold, their windows and gables decorated with fancy carvings in, of all things, the Jacobean Renaissance style.

Address Shipstone's Brewery, Radford Road, New Basford, Nottingham, NG7 7EA |
Getting there Tram to Shipstone Street, then a two-minute walk | Hours Visible from
outside only; no general access as such, but most of the brewery is now occupied by John
Pye Auctions (www.johnpye.co.uk) | Tip The Star Brewery may have closed, but filling the
alcoholic void is the excellent Black Iris Brewery, located a couple of minutes' walk away,
opposite the Shipstone Street tram stop (www.blackirisbottleshop.co.uk). Their pocket-
sized brewery tap, comprising several shelters in their yard, is open just two days a week:
Fri 4–8pm, Sat noon–8pm.

86 Smalleys

An excellent gentleman's outfitters

Half-way up Derby Road, one of Nottingham's main arteries, is a long and handsome, three- and four-storey red-brick terrace dating from the 1880s. As so often with Nottingham's Victorian buildings, it's the detail that delights, from the perky dormer windows through to the hooped stonework, shallow pilasters and terracotta tiling. All are signs of the era's self-confidence – and no wonder: the main architect, Samuel Dutton Walker (1833–1885), won a string of commissions in the city, lucrative enough for him to accumulate a small fortune by the time of his death.

Here, amidst this terrace, behind an inviting, dark-green shop front, you'll find Smalleys, a 'gentleman's outfitters' par excellence. The owner-proprietor is the charming Brandon Harris, who has presided over all things stylish for over 20 years. Brandon has long had a passion for suits. As a young man, he worked in the men's department at Harrods, where he admired the classic suit, shirt and tie look – so much so that he now has an extraordinary personal collection of several thousand ties and over 200 suits.

Brandon's personal items are not for sale – though he is always immaculately dressed – but the shop is packed to the gunnels with almost everything you can think of in terms of male attire, including shoes and ties, shirts, hats and assorted accessories, from belts and braces through to watches, both modern and vintage. One of the great pleasures here is that there's nothing neat and trim about the way the stock is displayed, and you're effectively invited to rummage to your heart's content – what a joy, as everything is top quality. Take the headwear, for example, piles of hats heaped and crowded together, from pork pies to traditional boaters, cowboy hats, and pretty much everything in between. At Smalleys – and this is a prime service – you can also be measured up and order a bespoke suit; they take between six and eight weeks to make.

Address 54 Derby Road, Nottingham, NG1 5FD, +44 (0)115 947 3853, www.smalleysgentsoutfitters.co.uk | **Getting there** Local bus (most lines) or tram to the city centre, then a five-minute walk | **Hours** Tue–Sat 11.30am–5.30pm | **Tip** If you're after ordering a bespoke suit, Smalleys may well be your best bet, but you could also check out one of their local rivals, British Tailoring, at 4 Derby Terrace (www.british-tailoring.com/nottingham-tailor).

87 __ Southwell Minster

One of England's most beautiful churches

Southwell, a well-heeled little town some 15 miles north-east of Nottingham, boasts one of the region's most beautiful buildings in Southwell Minster, where the main (west) façade is an exercise in symmetry, its twin towers topped by the dinkiest of pyramidal roofs, unique in all of England. The Normans built the Minster at the beginning of the 12th century and, although some elements were added later, their design predominates, from the towers of the west façade through to the dog-tooth decoration and the bull's-eye windows of the clerestory.

Inside, the proud and forceful nave, with its sturdy columns, marches up to the north transept, where there's an exquisite alabaster tomb of a long-forgotten churchman – Archbishop Sandys, who died in 1588. The red-flecked alabaster effigy of the bearded Sandys is so precise that you can see the furrows on his brow and the crow's feet round his eyes; his many children are depicted kneeling below, and it's assumed that Sandys was one of the first bishops to marry – and beget – after the break with Rome and the passage of Edward VI's Clergy Marriage Act in 1548. The nave's Norman stonework ends abruptly at the transepts with the inelegance of the 14th-century rood screen, beyond which lies the Early English choir and the remarkable chapter house, octagonal in shape and, unusually, without a central column. The chapter house is embellished with naturalistic foliage dating from the late 13th century, some of the earliest carving of its type in England; the plant species depicted are local, including oak, ivy, hawthorn and buttercup.

Outside the Minster, in an adjacent building, is the capacious State Chamber, with its splendid timber roof; this chamber, part of the Archbishop's Palace, was where Cardinal Wolsey (1473–1530) spent his last summer in royal disgrace after failing to secure Henry VIII a divorce from Catherine of Aragon.

Address Church Street, Southwell, NG25 0HD, +44 (0)1636 812649,
www.southwellminster.org | **Getting there** Bus to Southwell's Park Terrace, then a
10-minute stroll; if driving, there's a car park on the north side of the Minster, on
Church Street | **Hours** Mon–Sat 8.30am–6.30pm & Sun 8am–4.30pm | **Tip** For
food and drink, there are tasty offerings close by at the convivial Old Theatre Deli
(www.theoldtheatredeli.co.uk); try, for example, their delicious pea risotto.

88 Southwell Workhouse

UK's best-preserved workhouse

From a family of squires, parsons and slave traders, the Reverend John Thomas Becher (1770–1848) was a Southwell clergyman, who took a keen interest in social reform, but not from an excess of benevolence. Like many men of his class, he made a clear distinction between the 'deserving' and 'undeserving' poor – a distinction which guided him in his efforts to have a workhouse built for the relief of the destitute here in Southwell.

Becher's idea was that local parishes combine funds to build a workhouse, and the result was the large, three-storey brick structure that still stands on the edge of Southwell. Designed to resemble a prison and completed in 1824, it could hold 158 inmates, with adults divided into two categories: those unable to work ('blameless') and those capable of work ('idle and profligate able bodied'). Men, women and children were kept separate – so families could not meet – and most were made to work at some menial task; in return they were fed, clothed and housed.

Becher's harsh regime served as a blueprint for the multitude of workhouses which were soon to spring up across the country after the passing of the New Poor Law of 1834. In the event, these workhouses were to have a long life – the last vestiges of the Poor Law system hung around until the 1940s, and Southwell Workhouse was used as temporary accommodation for the homeless well into the 1970s.

The National Trust is now in possession of the property, and has returned the workhouse to an approximation of its original appearance, complete with infirmary, though this was only added to the workhouse in the 1870s. A series of displays explains the rules and regulations that once applied here and there are several discrete exhibits too, including The Women's Quilt, whose 598 patches commemorate women who were killed as a result of domestic violence between 2009 and 2015.

Address Upton Road, Southwell, NG25 0PT, +44 (0)1636 817260, www.nationaltrust.org.uk | Getting there Bus 26 from Nottingham stops at Chimes Meadow, a 10-minute walk away; if driving, there's a National Trust car park | Hours Mar–Jul & Sep–Oct, Wed–Sun 10.30am–4pm; Aug daily 10.30am–4pm | Tip From Southwell Workhouse, it's just four miles south to the hamlet of Thurgarton, where the Red Lion (www.redlionthurgarton.co.uk) is an outstanding gastropub – try, for example, the delicious rack of lamb.

89 Stained-glass at the Pitcher & Piano

A tasteful modernisation

Now the *Pitcher & Piano*, but once a bastion of Nonconformist liberal thinking, this former Unitarian Chapel cuts a dash at the west end of High Pavement, its splendid spire soaring high above its surroundings – and deliberately out-spiring St Mary's (see ch. 95), its religious rival, just along the street. There has been a church on this site since the late seventeenth century, but the present edifice went up in the 1870s, its size and generous neo-Gothic proportions reflecting both the wealth and tastes of its Victorian congregation. More recently, declining attendances prompted the closure of the church, which has now become a bar – the *Pitcher & Piano* – but the conversion was sympathetically done and the key features of the chapel respected.

The church's proudest feature is its stained glass, beginning with the luminous main window, a large and visually arresting affair whose 21 figures were the work of that wonderful pre-Raphaelite artist Edward Burne-Jones (1833–1898). Here, each of Burne-Jones's figures has a gentle elegance and each serves as a symbolic representation, from Labour and Theology through to Justice, Reverence and Mercy with the figure of Jesus with the Little Children as the exception. There's more delightful stained glass nearby in the north aisle, where two windows celebrate the centenary of the High Pavement Sunday School. These are floridly pre-Raphaelite windows, installed in 1906, the work of the prolific Henry Holiday (1839–1927), who knew Burne-Jones, succeeding him as a stained-glass window designer at a London glass works. Also in the north aisle is a two-window war memorial of 1925 featuring a brace of angels dressed in medieval armour in honour of two soldiers who lost their lives in World War I. These windows were designed by Charles Eamer Kempe (1837–1907), whose company specialised in stained glass windows, churning them out by the hundred.

Address *Pitcher & Piano*, High Pavement, Nottingham, NG1 1HN, +44 (0)115 958 6081, www.pitcherandpiano.com | Getting there Local bus (most lines) or tram to the city centre | Hours Daily noon – 11pm | Tip The sandstone under the centre of Nottingham is riddled with caves – and some of these can be explored at the City of Caves, a couple of minutes' walk from the Pitcher & Piano, at Garner's Hill, Nottingham, NG1 1HF (www.nationaljusticemuseum.org.uk/cityofcaves).

90__Standard Hill
'Charles Stuart, that man of blood'

Under windy skies, on Tuesday, 19 August, 1642, King Charles I planted his royal battle standard on Nottingham castle's tallest tower. He might have taken the hint when it blew down shortly afterwards, but instead he persevered, raising it again three days later on what is now Standard Hill – and in what is generally considered to the first act of the English Civil War.

Charles had been infuriated by Parliament's reluctance to grant him money to fund a war against the Scots, not to mention its attempts to limit royal power, but a wiser man would have noticed that Nottingham's townsfolk were not overly impressed by his shenanigans: the locals simply failed to rally to the royal cause and the king left the city in a grump with precious few new recruits. Such was his weakness that one of his aides, Jacob Astley, remarked that 'he could not give any assurance against his majesty being taken out of his [Nottingham] bed if any rebels should make such an attempt'. A modest plaque at the junction of Standard Hill and King Charles Street now marks the standard-raising spot.

In one of those curious twists of fate, the first English Civil War ended in Nottinghamshire too. In 1646, a deflated and defeated Charles I left Oxford in disguise to make his way on horseback to Southwell, 15 miles north-east of Nottingham, where he surrendered to the Scottish army that was besieging the Royalist stronghold of Newark. It wasn't, it should be noted, that Charles had a liking for the Scots, but rather he was hoping to exploit the rivalry that existed between his Scottish and English enemies. In the event, it didn't do him much good: the Scots soon handed him over to the English Parliamentary army and the king was executed in London on 30 January, 1649, a victim of his own duplicity as much as the animosity of his foes.

Address Standard Hill, Nottingham, NG1 6GL | Getting there Local bus (most lines) or tram to the city centre, then a five-minute walk | Hours Open access; free | Tip From Standard Hill , it's the briefest of strolls to what many consider to be the city's best hotel, Hart's (www.hartsnottingham.co.uk), which also boasts a first-rate and pleasantly informal restaurant.

91 St Barnabas Cathedral

Gothic revival delights by courtesy of Pugin

In the mid-19th century, a decade or so after the Emancipation Act removed most of the remaining restrictions against Roman Catholics, John Talbot, the Earl of Shrewsbury, dug into his very ample pockets to stump up the money to fund the construction of a Catholic church in Nottingham. The scheme was mostly the idea of a local priest, one Robert William Wilson (1794–1866), whose tireless work during an outbreak of cholera in the city in 1832 had made him both popular and influential.

The end result was the largest Catholic church built in England since the Reformation – completed in 1844 to a design by one of the most celebrated architects of the day, the prolific Augustus Pugin (1812–1852), who was flush with success after redesigning the Houses of Parliament in London. Pugin was the great proponent of Gothic Revival, and he stuck firmly to his architectural principles at St Barnabas, whose hulking stone exterior – very much in the Early English style – sports a rhythm of high gables that lead the eye to an imposing central tower and its turreted spire. The interior saw Pugin at his most flamboyant, but in an act of what can only be described as ecclesiastical vandalism, most of this interior work was destroyed in the 1960s.

Today much of the church is singularly dull, with acres of white paint and some of the most sentimental religious carvings imaginable. The exception is the charming Blessed Sacrament Chapel, not entirely the work of Pugin, but certainly in the Gothic Revival style, the bright and cheerful red, gold and green stencilling on its walls and arches culminating in an extravagantly detailed altar canopy, where angels stand guard. Late in the day, perhaps, but there are now plans to scrape off all the paint and restore Pugin's work, though it's not quite clear exactly what has survived, or whether the substantial cost can be justified.

Address North Circus Street, Nottingham, NG1 5AE, +44 (0)115 953 9839, www.stbarnabascathedral.org.uk | Getting there Local bus (most lines) or tram to the city centre | Hours Daily 8am–7pm | Tip St Barnabas also holds the tomb of a local nun, Mary Potter (1847–1913), the founder of a sisterly order, the Little Company of Mary, which is dedicated to tending to the sick and dying; the order has its headquarters in the city – and a local health centre is named after her.

92 St Margaret's Church

In Owthorpe, he 'threw off his ashes'

The hamlet of Owthorpe, around 12 miles south-east of Nottingham, is an unusual and pleasant little place, comprising little more than one street of pretty, red-brick cottages flanked by rolling pastureland. A grassy footpath leads off this street to the village's star turn, the church of St Margaret's, whose sturdy stonework dates back to the 13th century, though most of what you see today – including the tower – is from a rebuild commissioned in the 1650s by Colonel John Hutchinson (1615–1664).

This same Hutchinson, the local squire, fought for Parliament against the king during the Civil War, becoming the governor of Nottingham and then a regicide, just like Francis Hacker, his neighbour in Colston Bassett (see ch. 30). Unlike Hacker, however, Hutchinson avoided execution at the Restoration by repenting of his previous views, grovelling to say that Charles' execution was 'so horrid a crime as merits no indulgence'; such utterances helped save his neck, but gnawed away at his conscience until the day he died. Inside the church, a conspicuous wall monument bears tribute to the colonel in the form of a delightful rhyming poem (see above for a line taken from it), which was composed by his wife, Lucy Hutchinson (1620–1681). A remarkable woman, Lucy moved heaven and earth to stop her husband from being executed, but that's far from the whole story.

Lucy Hutchinson was a talented translator, poet and biographer, whose *Memoirs of the Life of Colonel Hutchinson* provide a real insight into the Civil War period. An ardent Puritan, Lucy was bitterly dismayed by the Restoration of Charles II, but still attended the king's triumphant entry into London when he was accompanied by the former parliamentary army in which she had invested such political hope. She could not fail to notice 'the mutability of some, the hypocrisy of others, and the servile flattery of all'.

Address St Margaret's church, Village Street, Owthorpe, Nottingham, NG12 3GA, +44 (0) 115 9892223, www.achurchnearyou.com/church/916 | **Getting there** No direct buses; around 30 minutes by car | **Hours** Services every second and fourth Sun of the month at 9am | **Tip** It's a little over two miles from ultra-quiet Owthorpe to small-town Cotgrave, where a large coal mine was opened in the 1960s. Many of the miners who worked Cotgrave were transferred here from the Northeast, but despite the large deposits of coal discovered, Cotgrave pit was still closed in 1994. Many a collier felt bitter and betrayed.

93 St Mary and St Hardulph

Who did the Breedon carvings? It's a mystery…

The ancient church of St Mary and St Hardulph is glued to the top of a heavily quarried hill just beyond the Nottinghamshire border. This was the site of a prehistoric hillfort, whose scant remains lie on the west side of the hill. Later, the kings of Mercia recognised Breedon's strategic importance by dispatching a band of monks to establish a priory here in the 7th century. The priory has disappeared in the mists of time, but the church you see today – a sturdy medieval structure with a chunky tower – has an especially intriguing interior.

To begin with, flanking the nave, there's the extravagant Shirley pew, a cage-like room within a room named after the family who bought the priory during the Reformation, and now inhabited by a trio of finely carved, 17th-century alabaster tombs. The grandest of these is a double decker, with a skeleton below and the Shirleys at prayer up above. Also edging the nave is an immaculately maintained Georgian box pew, but this is not nearly as rare as the Anglo-Saxon carvings scattered along the south side of the nave. Quite how they survived the turbulence of the Reformation is hard to say, but there are carvings of individual saints and angels, as well as wall friezes, where a dense foliage of vines encloses a tangle of animals and humans. Some of the figures, most memorably Mary and the saints positioned above the south-aisle altar, have drilled eyes into which were inserted precious stones; in the candle-lit interior of the Mercian priory this must have had an eerily dramatic effect.

Remarkably, the figures don't look Anglo-Saxon at all – witness Mary's three-fingered salutation with the fourth finger touching her thumb, a classic Byzantine pose; who the sculptors were and how they came to be here at this remote spot has fuelled much academic debate. Art historian Nikolaus Pevsner said the sculptures were 'inexplicable'.

Address Breedon on the Hill, Derby, DE 73 8AJ, www.breedonpriorychurch.org | Getting there By car, it's a 17-mile drive south-west from central Nottingham to Breedon on the Hill | **Hours** Daily 9.30am – 3.30pm | **Tip** The village of Breedon on the Hill is at the foot of the hill, the church is at the top; the most obvious way to travel between the two is along the narrow, gated and winding half-mile lane that begins in the village at The Green – just follow the signs. You can walk up the lane at any time, but cars can only use the lane during the daytime.

94___St Mary Magdalene
Newark's Dance of Death

Newark – more formally Newark-on-Trent – is an old and strate-gically important town on what was once the main route between north and south. Very different from its larger neighbour, big-city Nottingham, Newark has the feel of a market town, its intricate net-work of narrow lanes and alleys leading to the large and appealing Market Place. Footsteps from the Market Place, shoehorned into a surprisingly narrow space, is St Mary Magdalene, one of the region's grandest churches.

Three hundred years in the making from around 1220, the church is primarily an example of the Perpendicular Gothic, though the massive, tapering tower at the front is a mixture of styles – witness the Decorated Gothic blind arcading at its base. It is, however, the church's interior that impresses most. A platoon of architectural his-torians – including Simon Jenkins – have swooned over the superb proportions of the nave, which is supported by the slimmest and most elegant of piers. The transepts are equally bold, the windows as large as was structurally possible at the time, and the chancel is cheered by an enormous east window. Also in the chancel, just beyond the organ, is the cage-like Markham Chantry Chapel, where priests were paid to pray for Robert Markham, who died in 1506.

The chapel's stonework is not especially riveting, but, remarkably enough, two of its panels carry a rare 16th-century painting depict-ing the so-called 'Dance of Death': on one side, a grimacing skele-ton points to the ground and offers a carnation to a richly-dressed man on the other panel. Such pictorial warnings of mortality were not unusual in medieval times, but precious few survive, and this one is especially beautiful, executed in the brightest of colours, and with the sharpest of details, from the long and slender fingers of the skeleton, to the puffed-up, black- and white-striped sleeves of the gentleman.

Address Church Walk, Newark, NG24 1JS | Getting there Train to Newark Castle, then a 10-minute walk; by car, it's a 50-minute drive from Nottingham to Newark via Southwell and the A612 | Hours Mon–Sat 9am–3pm | Tip St Mary Magdalene is on the edge of Newark's Market Place, where the star architectural turn is the Town Hall, which boasts a splendid Neo-classical façade.

95 St Mary's Church

Nottingham's anti-slavery tombstone

St Mary's is the grandest church in Nottingham, its sleek and handsomely carved frame leading the eye to a sturdy stone tower, topped by eight pinnacles. There has been a church here since Saxon times, but what you see today is largely 15th-century, with the interior dappled by the light that filters through the stained-glass windows. And it's here in the nave, in Nottingham, one of England's most landlocked counties, that there's a real surprise: the tomb of a certain Lieutenant James Still, who died of yellow fever off the coast of West Africa at the tender age of 22.

The British led the way in developing the Atlantic slave trade between Britain, Africa and the Americas, but for various reasons – some genuinely humanitarian – the British Parliament banned the trade by passing the Slave Trade Act in 1807. The British then hammered home the point by interrupting the whole of the Atlantic slave trade, and for 50 years the Royal Navy patrolled what was then known as the 'Slave Coast' of West Africa, intercepting slave ships bound for the Americas. Admittedly, the Royal Navy skimped on resources and the sailors didn't much like the posting – it was monotonous, very hot and tropical diseases were a constant threat – but nevertheless the British did capture 1,600 slave ships and free 150,000 slaves over these 50 years. Most were shipped as free men and women to the British colony of Sierra Leone.

It was during this time that Lieutenant Still met his maker but, with much of British history so steeped in slavery, it's heart-warming to read the tributes to the lieutenant alongside a heartfelt condemnation of the trade – this 'traffick in human blood'. Lieutenant Still was on the HMS Pheasant, an 18-gun sloop, whose proudest moment came in 1821 when it stopped the Portuguese slaver Adelaide from proceeding, liberating 230 slaves in the process. Slavery was finally banned in the British Empire in the 1830s.

Address High Pavement, Nottingham, NG1 1HN, www.stmarysnottingham.org | **Getting there** Local bus (most lines) or tram to the city centre, then a five-minute walk | **Hours** Opening hours vary – see website for current information on visiting; free | **Tip** Don't forget St Mary's angels: look up into the roof of the nave and you'll spy 10 golden angels. These finely carved, oak figures were always hard to spot, but in 2023 they were restored and gilded – to the congregation's delight.

96 Stonebridge City Farm

An award-winning City Farm

There's something really rather charming about Stonebridge City Farm. A charity with the most heart warming of objectives, it comprises a mini-farm and community facility located in St Ann's, an inner-city part of Nottingham, where modern council houses jostle with one-time textile factories and warehouses. In the 1960s and '70s, the old terraces of St Ann's were demolished to make way for modern housing. As part of the regeneration, a school was planned for Stonebridge Road, but it proved surplus to requirements and the land became derelict. Then, in the 1970s, the newly founded British City Farm Movement provided inspiration for the creation of a city farm here: a lease was signed for the site in 1978, and a barn erected two years later.

Stonebridge has expanded over the years, with most visitors now bringing their children to gaze at and / or feed an assortment of cows, goats, sheep, pigs and horses – bags of animal food are available to buy. These animals roam the paddocks behind the main buildings, where the barn holds smaller, petting animals, such as guinea pigs and rabbits, and also the noble Kevin, an ancient and strangely handsome 8.5kg tortoise.

Other notable residents include an aviary of exotic birds, plus ducks, turkeys, geese and chickens, which provide a bountiful supply of eggs. Stonebridge has also tried its hand at bee-keeping, and one section has been cultivated with vegetable plots, orchards and greenhouses. Locals can drop their pet rabbits and guinea pigs off here when they go on holiday. The animals are well looked after by over 100 volunteers, many of whom have a mental health challenge or learning disability. These same volunteers help in the running of the café, picking up essential life skills as they go. The pleasure these volunteers take in tending to the animals is a pleasure to behold.

Address Stonebridge Road, Nottingham, NG3 2FR, +44 (0)115 950 5113, www.stonebridgecityfarm.com | **Getting there** Local bus (most lines) or tram to the city centre, then a 15-minute walk; alternatively, bus 25 or 26 to St Chads Road, and a three-minute walk | **Hours** Daily 10am–3pm; entrance is free, but donations are appreciated | **Tip** Stonebridge Farm is unique in the city; if you want to upgrade to a zoo, the nearest good one is Twycross Zoo (www.twycrosszoo.org), 30 miles away in Leicestershire.

97 The Stone Monkey

Watson Fothergill primate holds the purse strings

A devotee of the Gothic Revival style of architecture and a leading local luminary, Watson Fothergill (1841–1928) was a busy and popular architect here in Nottingham. During his long career, Fothergill designed no fewer than five banks, commissions that netted him a fair slab of money – and one of the reasons why he died a very rich man.

The pick of the five, completed in 1882 as the headquarters of the long-defunct Nottingham and Nottinghamshire Bank, dominates Thurland Street, just off the Market Square. The centrepiece of this particular edifice is a high and mighty stone tower very much in the Flemish / Rhenish style, with a set of decorative turrets just below the spire. Down below, the main façade extends right along the street, balustraded at the top and with two main sets of Gothic-style windows, a corner turret, mini-friezes, decorative balconies and elongated chimneys – though the most southerly section was added in a matching style in the 1920s.

Inside, the old banking hall is a handsome, circular affair with a stately dome supported on marble columns. One of these columns sports a stone monkey, whose left hand holds a chain, which appears to be attached to a wad of paper money. There has been some debate as to the meaning of the monkey, but the animal once looked out over customers queueing to do business at the counter, a timely warning, perhaps, not to get enchained by the bank at a time when a mortgage was commonly called a 'stone monkey'.

As far as the Nottingham and Nottinghamshire Bank was concerned, Fothergill was certainly right to give a warning: a few years after the bank's headquarters were completed, it was discovered that one of its managers had defrauded the bank of £25,000 (equivalent to around £3 million in today's money); the manager couldn't be prosecuted, however, as he had drowned himself by jumping into the River Trent.

Address 2–3 Thurland Street, Nottingham, NG1 3DR | **Getting there** Local bus (most lines) or tram to the city centre | **Hours** The interior of the building has been turned into the BOX bar daily noon–midnight (www.theboxbar.co.uk). | **Tip** The large and really rather handsome, red-brick and stone-trimmed building across Thurland Street from Fothergill's creation is the former Corn Exchange, which was completed in the 1850s to a design by T. C. Hine.

98__St Stephen's Choir Stalls
Fancy, folkloric medieval carving

Fanning out from the eastern edge of the city centre, Sneinton has preserved something of a separate identity, a multicultural, inner-city quarter whose Victorian and more modern terraced houses curl their way up and over a gentle ridge. It's here, surrounded by its extensive graveyard, that you'll find St Stephen's, which – with its lancet-style windows – is reckoned to be the first manifestation of the neo-Gothic in the county. There's actually been a church here since the middle of the 13th century, but the present structure, including its chunky, sooty clock tower, dates from the 1830s. There's no mistaking this is High Church Anglicanism territory too: the unusual war memorial in the graveyard displays Christ on the Cross above a remembrance tablet to the dead of World War I – an unusual combination in (Protestant) England.

The interior of the church holds a bright and cheerful, finely detailed reredos (above the high altar), the work of Cecil Greenwood Hare (1875–1932). Hare specialised in such Gothic Revival extravagances, and was also the man responsible for the church's Calvary War Memorial. Yet the highlight – and the real reason for a visit – is the church's set of wooden choir stalls, which date from the 15th century. They were actually made for St Mary's (see ch. 95), in the city centre, but were thrown out and subsequently salvaged by an enterprising clergyman in 1848.

Sixty years later, they were modified to fit into the space behind St Stephen's rood screen. Flip up any of the choir seats, and you'll find the most fascinating of misericord carvings, folkloric and distinctly secular scenes, such as a cat with a mouse in its mouth, a bearded head, a chained ape, and this author's personal favourite, a fox blowing a hunting horn whilst riding a hound, which itself looks positively unhinged – as in the world turned upside down, an irreligious, sometimes radical view of a regimented, hierarchical society.

Address Dale Street, Nottingham, NG2 4JN, www.achurchnearyou.com/church/17954 | **Getting there** Local bus (most lines) or tram to the city centre, then a 20-minute walk; alternatively, bus to Windmill Lane, a few yards from the church | **Hours** Thu & Sun 9.30am–noon | **Tip** Sneinton was a centre of high church Anglicanism from the 1860s to the 1930s. Five churches were built or remodelled during this period and – apart from St Stephens – the most interesting is the neo-Byzantine St Cyprian on Marston Road (www.stcyprian.org.uk).

99 Theatre Royal

Nottingham's main concert hall

Proud and really rather grand, the Theatre Royal peers out over Nottingham, down towards the Market Square, its six tall and slender Corinthian pillars punctuating a handsome façade that sports the city's coat of arms. Completed in 1865, the money for the theatre came from a local lace manufacturer, and the architect was Charles John Phipps (1835–1897), whose stellar career designing a brigade of British theatres made him rich and famous, though his last years were scarred by scandal: in 1887, the Theatre Royal he had built in Exeter caught fire, killing 186 people, and the ensuing inquiry was deeply critical of his design.

With the Exeter fire in mind, Nottingham's Theatre Royal was partly remodelled in the 1890s, the first of several reworkings as the theatre's fortunes saw considerable fluctuation. By the late 1960s, however, the place was in a sorry state – so much so that the dressing rooms were reckoned to be the worst in the country. Then, like a fairy godmother in one of the theatre's pantos, in stepped the city council – 'Oh, yes they did!' – and stumped up the money for a grand refurbishment. In a bold move they commissioned a combination of architects: one lot known for its modernist leanings, the other, led by Iain Mackintosh, keen to restore and retain historic theatres.

Perhaps surprisingly, the two sets of architects worked well together and the result is a delight, beginning with the spacious foyer and a grand staircase that spirals up to one of the theatre's bars. Beyond, in the auditorium, the seating is banked up with three tiers of horseshoe-shaped galleries perched on columns, whose design mirrors that of the main façade. Today, the Theatre Royal offers a popular and varied programme of plays, opera, ballet, musicals and pantos. It works in conjunction with the adjacent Royal Concert Hall, a larger auditorium, completed in 1982, which occupies a modern building to the rear.

Address Theatre Square, Nottingham, NG1 5ND, box office +44 (0)115 989 5555, www.trch.co.uk | **Getting there** Local bus (most lines) or tram to the city centre | **Hours** Variable; see website for current information on performances and backstage tours | **Tip** From the Theatre Royal, it's the briefest of strolls to the open-air delights of the Market Square, site of a winter festival and a summertime (sandy) beach.

100_ Tough Mary's Bakehouse
The best bread, cakes and croissants in town

Sloping up to Canning Circus from the city centre, the first part of Derby Road was meant to impress, its grand, Victorian red-brick terraces equipped with capacious ground-floor windows to better display the wares of the street's upmarket shops and stores. Inevitably, there have been some unfortunate modern additions to this streetscape – take the (now defunct) Strathdon Hotel as an example – but more than enough remains to recall past aspirations, including the handsome terrace at nos. 48-60, with its dinky dormer windows, decorative tiling and neo-classical pilasters.

This particular block was completed in 1873, at roughly the same time as the architect Gilbert Smith Doughty (1861–1909) chimed in with a good-looking, Flemish-influenced terrace at nos. 70–82. What's more, it's here, at 70–72, that you'll find Tough Mary's Bakehouse, which many reckon to be the best bakery in town. It's certainly popular, and if you visit on a Saturday morning there's a good chance you'll have to join a very long queue.

Tough Mary's occupies two adjacent premises – one is the bakery, where you can peep in through the window and see what's happening; the other has the counter and a bright and cheerful mini-café with a handful of tables. All the food they sell is made from raw ingredients, and they always avoid improvers or additives. Their most popular loaves are sourdough – white, seeded and rye, for instance – and they also bake ciabatta and vegan baguettes.

The puffy croissants – memorably the Cinnamon Croissant Monster – are really tempting, as are the really rather exotic peanut, date and chocolate bars and the doughnuts. But this author's favourite is the banana bread, which must be the best north of the Alps. Most customers do take away, with many ordering online beforehand, but if you do sit down, a great hot chocolate and fine range of teas are on offer.

Address 70-72 Derby Road, Nottingham, NG1 5FD, +44 (0)115 837 4321, www.toughmarysbakehouse.co.uk | **Getting there** 5- to 10-minute walk from the city centre | **Hours** Tue–Fri 8.30am–3pm, Sat 9.30am–3pm | **Tip** Tough Mary's Bakehouse may be the best café in town, but it has its rivals, like Blend (www.blendnottingham.co.uk), which has one of its three branches nearby at the foot of Derby Road – and the west end of Parliament Street; what's more, you're much more likely to get a seat at Blend than you are at Tough Mary's.

101 Trent Bridge Cricket Ground

'A lotus land for batsmen,' said Neville Cardus

One of the most famous cricket grounds in the world, Trent Bridge is a handsome affair, its assorted terraces overlooking an immaculately maintained, grassy-green outfield, which itself surrounds the browning strips of the cricket pitches. In recent decades, the ground has experienced several redevelopments, some more successful than others. The Victorian pavilion has survived in good condition, however, its mottled-brick chimneys and bright-white wooden galleries home to the members' facilities and players' dressing rooms.

Trent Bridge has witnessed some of the sport's finest moments, from the imperious century Donald Bradman notched up here in the 1948 Ashes, to the remarkable 8 wickets for 15 runs taken by fast bowler Stuart Broad against the Australians in 2015. What made Broad's success so much sweeter was that he was born in Nottingham – and indeed, Broad was but the latest in a long line of local bowlers to have achieved fame if not necessarily fortune here.

The old cliché was that if you whistled down the pit shaft at any Nottinghamshire coal mine, you'd find a fast bowler – and such a man was Harold Larwood (1904–1995), one of the greatest and fastest of all time. Born in Nuncargate, around 14 miles north of Nottingham, Larwood went down the pit at the age of 14, but his talents had been spotted: by 1924 he was playing for Nottinghamshire Cricket Club, and two years later he was selected for England. All seemed set fair, but Larwood was used to intimidate Bradman and his fellow Australians in the notorious 'Bodyline' tour of 1932–33, in which Larwood's short pitched bowling scared his opponents half to death. In one way it worked – England won the Ashes – but it created an international incident of which Larwood was the sacrificial goat: he never played for England again.

Address Trent Bridge, West Bridgford, Nottingham, NG2 6AG, www.trentbridge.co.uk | Getting there Local bus (several lines) from the city centre direct to Trent Bridge | Hours Trent Bridge cricket ground is open for a variety of cricket matches and there are also occasional guided tours – see website for more information | Tip It's a brief walk from the Trent Bridge cricket ground to an excellent pub, the Stratford Haven (www.castlerockbrewery.co.uk).

102 University of Nottingham
Art, architecture and archaeology

For many years, the immensely wealthy Jesse Boot (1850–1931), of Boots the Chemist, was the principal benefactor of Nottingham University, and it was down to his efforts that today's University Park Campus, the main campus, occupies an attractively landscaped, moderately hilly tract of land about three miles south-west of the city centre. The university moved here in 1928, and for many years afterwards eschewed modern architecture in the construction of its various buildings, opting instead for an appealing if somewhat sedate classicism that remains the dominant theme of the core of the campus today. The most successful structure is perhaps the 1928 Trent Building, with its long stone façade and Italianate tower, whereas the Portland Building, finished in 1956, is less successful, undone by its overpowering portico.

The Trent Building looks out across the Highfields Park Boating Lake and Lakeside Arts, the umbrella name for a group of buildings that offer both performing arts and temporary exhibitions. The best known of these venues is undoubtedly the Djanogly Art Gallery, whose exhibitions showcase 20th-century and contemporary art; many have received top-notch reviews and all are supported by public lectures.

Less well known is the pint-sized Archaeology Museum, which showcases a surprisingly interesting range of local artefacts from prehistoric to medieval times, though its speciality is a collection of Samian Roman pottery. Similarly unfamiliar is the Weston Gallery, in the D. H. Lawrence Pavilion, where a regularly rotated selection of documents and manuscripts drawn from the university's collection is on display. Other spaces include the Djanogly Theatre and the Djanogly Recital Hall – and, just in case you wondered who this 'Djanogly' is, well, it's Sir Harry Arieh Simon Djanogly (born 1938), who made his fortune in Nottingham textiles.

Address Lakeside Arts, University Park, Nottingham, NG7 2RD, +44 (0)115 846 7777, www.lakesidearts.org.uk | **Getting there** Tram to University of Nottingham, then a three-minute walk to Lakeside Arts | **Hours** Djanogly Art Gallery Tue–Sat 10am–4pm & Sun noon–4pm; Weston Gallery Tue–Sun noon–4pm; University of Nottingham Archaeology Museum Thu–Sun noon–4pm | **Tip** If Lakeside Arts feels a little high-brow and serious, then relief is at hand: Highfields Park has its own crazy golf course (yippee!) and you can rent out a variety of canoes and boats to sally out into the lake.

103 Warhammer World

Gamers' paradise – maybe even Valhalla

A mystery to non-gamers perhaps, but there's no denying that Nottingham-based Games Workshop (GW) has provided a real boost to the city's economy. From modest beginnings in the 1970s, the company has vaulted its rivals to become the largest and most successful hobby miniatures company in the world, with substantial overseas sales. The heart of their business is the design and manufacture of fantastical miniature soldiers, which gamers then use in battle. The soldiers draw on all sorts of tropes for their appearance, mostly from science fiction, and many – like the orcs – are extraordinarily savage-looking.

GW also produces lots of supplementary material, such as model-painting kits, miniature fighting vehicles, fantasy novels, and detailed rule books – gamers take these battles very seriously indeed. The company's two big sellers are Warhammer and Warhammer 40,000, the latter currently being the most popular miniature wargame in the world. GW also holds the licence for The Lord of the Rings / The Hobbit battle game.

GW's expansive headquarters are in Lenton, around three miles west of the city centre. Here, perched on a plinth outside the main office, GW announces itself with a life-sized, fully armed and armoured Warhammer figure. Close by, in another building, is Warhammer World, which attracts enthusiastic gamers from far and wide; it's guarded by the figure of a Space Marine, who can, apparently, 'shoot any enemy unit within 24 inches' with his 'boltgun'. Inside, a store sells lots of gamers' stuff, four exhibition arenas feature Warhammer scenarios, and there's a large Gaming Hall, where intense gamers do battle within the hall's imitation, castle-like walls. There's a further dollop of neo-medievalism in the café-restaurant, Bugman's, which has heavy-duty wooden furnishings and fittings, and even knights' helmets on the mantel above the fireplace.

Address Willow Road, Lenton, Nottingham, NG7 2WS, +44 (0)115 900 4151, www.warhammer.com | Getting there Tram to Gregory Street, then a 5- to 10-minute walk | Hours Sun–Wed 10am–6pm, Thu & Fri 10am–10pm, Sat 10am–8pm | Tip For a gentler introduction to the gamer universe, you might try GW's much smaller city centre premises, Warhammer World, at 34A Friar Lane.

104 Watson Fothergill Offices

Gothic revival architecture at its best

Born in Mansfield, the son of a wealthy lace manufacturer, Watson Fothergill (1841–1928) was the most prolific of architects, designing over 100 buildings in and around Nottingham, over the course of a career that spanned around four decades. There were banks and warehouses, offices, churches and private houses – and almost always Fothergill plumped for an elaborate, often playful, version of the Gothic Revival style. This, in its turn, was broadly based on surviving Tudor buildings and medieval churches.

All in all, Fothergill did much to define the appearance of Victorian and Edwardian Nottingham at a time when it was in the throes of an economic boom. In the 1720s, Daniel Defoe had observed that Nottingham was 'pleasant and beautiful,' but by the 1850s this old market town had been transformed into a major industrial city.

A string of Watson Fothergill buildings has survived and, although some are now looking rather battered and bruised, the offices he built for himself on George Street in the 1890s survive in fine fettle. The façade of this structure sports contrasting horizontal bands of red and blue brick, one of Fothergill's most popular devices, as well as hooped windows and a delightful corner turret-tower, with a candlesnuffer roof and a brace of dinky dormer windows. In a burst of playfulness, Fothergill added a statue of a medieval figure, who appears to be studying some architectural plan or another – but the face may in fact be that of Fothergill himself.

Just above this statue are several pint-sized stone busts, including one of Augustus Pugin (1812–1852), the pioneering architect who took the lead in developing the Gothic Revival style. There's also one of Norman Shaw (1831–1912), a talented Scottish architect who built his reputation on the redesign of several country houses and numerous commercial buildings.

Address 15 George Street, Nottingham, NG1 3BU | Getting there Local bus (most lines) or tram to city centre, then a five-minute walk | Hours Always visible, from outside only | Tip Just up and along George Street from Fothergill's old offices is the Nottingham Arts Theatre (www.nottingham-theatre.co.uk), where the emphasis is on supporting and encouraging young talent in the performing arts.

105 — Welbeck Abbey
Medieval abbey turned aristocratic estate

What's in a name? The owners of Welbeck Abbey seem to hyphenate their surnames at the drop of a hat, the result of all sorts of comings and goings that stretch out into the distant past. They are also very rich. When Lady Anne Cavendish-Bentinck (1916 – 2008) died, she not only owned the sprawling Welbeck Abbey estate, but also a treasure trove of paintings by the likes of Stubbs and van Dyck.

The most famous of the clan, however, was the 5th Duke of Portland (1800 – 1879), known as the 'burrowing duke' for the maze of gaslit tunnels he constructed beneath his estate. Naturally enough, many people thought he was bonkers, but the truth may well be more complex. This is an issue explored in Mick Jackson's novel *The Underground Man*, wherein the duke is portrayed as a shy man haunted by his obsessions. Others have attributed his burrowing down to the disfiguring effects of a skin disease.

The duke's tunnels are not open to the public, which is a real shame, and although there are occasional guided tours of Welbeck's state rooms, most of the estate is off limits most of the time. That said, there has been some relaxation in recent years, and a few of Welbeck's buildings are now occupied by small businesses, with others being used as film sets: Nicolas Refn's *Bronson* was partly shot in the massive underground ballroom here in 2008 – indeed, this author was an extra, though blink and you might miss his contribution.

Today, Welbeck's key attractions are on the western edge of the estate, where the old Victorian gas works has been turned into the Harley Gallery, with a top-of-the-range gift shop on the ground floor and temporary exhibitions above. The Harley also offers a range of classes and workshops. A sleek new building next door houses the Portland Collection, which showcases items from the family's private collection, from portraits, timepieces and rare books, through to silverware, jewellery and paintings.

Address Harley Gallery at the Welbeck Estate, Welbeck, Worksop, S 80 3LW, +44 (0)1909 501 700, www.harleyfoundation.org.uk | **Getting there** By car, it's a 28-mile drive north from Nottingham to the Harley Gallery and the Portland Collection via the A 614/A 616 | **Hours** Harley Gallery & the Portland Collection Tue – Sun 10am – 4pm; guided tours of Welbeck Abbey's state rooms must be booked in advance via www.welbeck.co.uk; Welbeck Farm Shop Mon – Sat 9am – 5pm & Sun 9am – 4pm | **Tip** The Harley Art Trail, beginning beside the Harley Gallery, leads out across the surrounding countryside to reach – after around 25 minutes – Creswell Crags, a limestone gorge with a scattering of prehistoric rock carvings (www.creswell-crags.org.uk).

106 __ Wild Clothing
Great vintage clothing pick and mix

In Nottingham, many fashion roads lead back to Paul Smith (see ch. 74) and this is certainly the case with Wild Clothing, easily the city's best vintage clothing store. It was founded back in the 1980s by two groovy lads – Robin Pounder and Miles Oakley – who hatched their entrepreneurial plans whilst working at Smith's Nottingham store. Their hunch was that there was a gap in the market for vintage clothing – and so it proved, with the duo initially specialising in handpicked items from the 1940s to the 1960s, principally from the USA and the UK. Oakley and Pounder had a canny eye for vintage – indeed, they kept this author supplied with fantastic Hawaiian shirts for well over a decade – and as time went by so they added items from the 1970s through to the 1990s.

Wild Clothing sits at the very centre of The Hockley, Nottingham's most fashionable quarter, and inside the store's crowded rails are laden with a wide range of items for both men and women, ranging from shirts to coats, blouses to dresses, hats, shoes and even, on occasion, old and luridly coloured roller skates. Most of the stock is displayed on the ground floor, but a sturdy wooden staircase leads down to a basement section, where yet more vintage goodies can be found.

In recent years, the shop has experienced tough trading conditions, changing hands in 2020 and again in 2023, but the new owners – Charlotte Oaten and Rob Hague – have revitalized the shop whilst keeping its alternative vibe. They have also added several new and interesting clothing brands, widened the range of their suppliers and continue to do a great line in vintage denim – and vintage vinyl. Incidentally, for something entirely different, you can pop across the street to Void. This is another clothing store, also established in the 1980s, but here the emphasis is very much on 'Alternative' (read Goth / Heavy Metal) clothing – so no Hawaiian shirts here then.

Address 4–6 Broad Street, Nottingham, NG1 3AL, +44 (0)115 941 3928 | Getting there Local bus (most lines) or tram to the city centre, then a five-minute walk | Hours Mon–Sat 10am–6pm, Sun 11am–4pm | Tip From Wild Clothing, it's the shortest of walks to what many consider to be the best pizza place in town, *Slice 'n Brew* (www.slicenbrew.co.uk), in bright, modern premises at 10 King's Walk.

107 __ Wilford Suspension Bridge

The prettiest way to traverse the Trent

Completed in 1906, Wilford Suspension Bridge is one of Nottingham's grandest structures, its twin stone towers and supporting steel cables creating a graceful 69-metre span over the River Trent. Perhaps surprisingly, given the imposing nature of the bridge, it was originally built as an aqueduct rather than a transport link, its use confined to walkers – and more latterly cyclists – who mostly employ it as a shortcut from the Meadows to West Bridgford. On the bridge, the old metal grills that stop people tumbling into the river have accumulated scores of little padlocks, left here by all and sundry. While not particularly original – other bridges have the same padlock decoration – it's pleasantly folksy nonetheless.

Strolling along the east bank of the river from the Suspension Bridge, you soon spy Trent Bridge, whose granite cutwater columns and cast-iron arches date from the 1870s. The bridge was designed by the city engineer of the time, the splendidly named Marriott Ogle Tarbotton (1834–1887), who was well respected for his efforts to make the city healthier, culverting streams and overseeing the construction of an underground sewerage system – the first in England outside London. Almost nothing remains of the medieval stone bridge that pre-dates the existing structure, but a couple of its arches have survived in a grassy hollow in the middle of the road at the bridge's east end.

Curiously enough, during the riots that spread across much of England in 1981, staff from Nottinghamshire County Council's Youth Service were asked to guard both Wilford Suspension Bridge and Trent Bridge: there were rumours that the working-class youngsters of the Meadows were about to invade middle-class West Bridgford. It was all nonsense, of course, and the bemused youth workers proceeded to do absolutely nothing.

Address Wilford Suspension Bridge, West Bridgford, Nottingham, NG2 7TA | Getting there Bus to Trent Bridge, then a 10-minute walk | Hours Open access; free | Tip Yards from the west side of the Wilford Suspension Bridge is Victoria Embankment, whose Memorial Gardens incorporate manicured gardens and ornamental pools as well as a grand Memorial Arch, completed in the 1920s to commemorate the dead of World War I.

108__William Booth Halls
Salvation Army's local HQ

Completed in 1915, the William Booth Memorial Halls take their name from William Booth, the founder of the Salvation Army, who was born here in the city in 1829. Moved by the poverty he saw around him – and his own family's descent into penury – Booth started out as a Methodist lay preacher, but that didn't satisfy his soul, and he went on to found a Christian Mission dedicated to helping the poor and needy. In a moment of what he considered to be divine inspiration, Booth chanced upon the name 'Salvation Army', founding, in 1878, an evangelical organisation whose volunteers soon adopted a quasi-military uniform, which they continue to sport today.

The Memorial Halls, which still serve as the local headquarters of the Salvation Army, are of neo-classical design, the red brick and stone-trimmed exterior culminating in a distinctive, copper-domed tower. Inside, the main Meeting Hall is a pleasant space with detailed plasterwork and a panelled balcony all to a design by Oswald Archer, who was the Salvation Army's go-to architect for nigh-on 30 years. Various modifications have been made since construction, but there's a notable lack of religious symbolism, with the front of the Meeting Hall (where you might anticipate an altar) adorned by a portrait of William Booth with flags to either side. Booth made himself 'General' for life, passing the title down to his son, William Bramwell Booth (1856–1929), who laid one of the foundation stones on the outside of the building, which survives intact.

Incidentally, if you pop over to the foyer of the Broadway Cinema (see ch. 20), just a five-minute walk away, you'll spy an ornate plaque that celebrates Booth's 'conversion' to Christianity in what was at the time a Methodist chapel. The Salvation Army continues to play a key role as a charity both in the UK and across the globe.

Address 7 King Edward Street, Nottingham, NG1 1EU, www.salvationarmy.org.uk |
Getting there Local bus (most lines) or tram to the city centre, then a five-minute walk |
Hours Opening hours vary – see website for current information on visiting; free | Tip
From the Memorial Halls, it's a 10-minute walk to the modest William Booth Birthplace
Museum at 14 Notintone Street (www.salvationarmy.org.uk).

109 Wollaton Hall

Breath-taking in its invention

One of the finest Elizabethan mansions in the country, Wollaton Hall sits on top of a grassy knoll in the middle of a large deer park. The architectural sensation of its day, it was built in the 1580s for Francis Willoughby (1546–1596), who had made a fortune from his coal mines, and designed by Robert Smythson. The mansion's façade is an exercise in flamboyant symmetry, its sandy-coloured stonework intercepted by turrets and chimneys, niches and medallions, friezes and balustrades, all of which serve to frame a veritable ocean of glass.

Inside, the Great Hall, with an imposing stone screen, is the most authentic room in the house, but be sure to climb the spiral stairs to the capacious Prospect Room, from where there are magnificent views. Otherwise, little remains of Smythson's original interior, reflecting Wollaton Hall's chequered fortunes: damaged by fire, sometimes abandoned and occasionally remodelled, the owners rarely took to the place and ultimately sold it to the City Council in 1924. The Council installed a Natural History Museum and this still makes for a popular family outing, though there have been some changes in perspective: visitors of a certain vintage, like this author, will remember George, a stuffed gorilla, who struck a ferocious pose at the museum's entrance; George has survived, but now he looks much more relaxed in a mock-up of his jungle environment.

At the back of the house, and protected by a ha-ha (the animal-excluding ditch and low wall), are well-tended formal gardens as well as the Camellia House, a recently restored cast-iron glass house dating back to the 1820s. Nearby, at the side of the house, a large block of 18th-century stables and agricultural buildings holds a modest Industrial Museum and from here footpaths lead across the park; the obvious target is the lake with its woods and encircling footpath.

Address Wollaton Road, Nottingham, NG8 2AE, +44 (0)115 876 3100, www.wollatonhall.org.uk | **Getting there** Bus to the Rectory Gardens beside the main entrance to Wollaton Hall, on Wollaton Road | **Hours** Hall and Industrial Museum open daily 11am–4pm; Prospect Room open only on Hidden History guided tours, bookable either online or in person at the Hall; gardens open daily 9am–4pm; park open Mon–Fri 8am–dusk, Sat & Sun 9am–dusk | **Tip** Wollaton Hall's architect was the talented and prolific Robert Smythson, who also designed Longleat in Wiltshire and Hardwick Hall (see ch. 43).

110 World War I Memorial

Nottingham High School honours its dead

Nottingham High School, founded in 1513 by Dame Agnes Mellers, a Tudor benefactor of whom little is known, lays fair claim to be the best public school in the region. Initially, the High School occupied premises in the city centre, but moved to its present location – bordered by Arboretum Street to the south and Forest Road to the north – in the 1860s. Since then, the school has gradually expanded to fill almost the entire block with, for example, the Player Hall, of broadly Gothic design, added in the 1930s, and a Science Block constructed in the 1980s.

Nottingham High School – Nottingham High School for Boys until it went co-educational in 2015 – is seen to best advantage from Arboretum Street. From here there's a fine view of the school's original Victorian façade, a sweeping stone structure, two- and three-storeys high, adorned by neo-Jacobean detailing and fronted by well-tended grounds. In the middle, the façade is intercepted by an imposing tiered and turreted tower equipped with a flagpole, atop of which a flag flutters on special occasions. The flight of stone steps leading into the tower was once the preserve of Sixth Formers and staff, but these precise rules and regulations were relaxed years ago – as were others about boys having to wear shorts and caps.

In front of this stone façade is a dramatic World War I Memorial featuring a life-sized bronze of an officer beckoning his men forward from the top of a plinth. You can tell he's an officer from his uniform and the holster at his thigh: only officers were permitted pistols. The monument was unveiled in 1921 by a local veteran and dignitary, Lieutenant Colonel Brewill. The school would surely have preferred its most celebrated military hero, the fighter ace Albert Ball, V.C., to have presided – but unfortunately Ball crashed and died in France in 1917, at the tender age of 20.

Address Waverley Mount, Nottingham, NG7 4ED | Getting there Tram to the 'High School' stop, then a three-minute walk | Hours The War Memorial is visible at any time through the school's iron fence on Arboretum Street | Tip Nottingham High School shares Arboretum Street with another public school, the Nottingham Girls' High School; now that both establishments take girls, the rivalry is intense.

111 Ye Olde Trip to Jerusalem

The oldest inn in the land – well maybe

The infinitely quaint Ye Olde Trip to Jerusalem, sitting pretty at the foot of the sandstone cliff that clambers up to Nottingham Castle, may well be England's oldest inn, though the title is hotly disputed. Legend has it that the Crusaders assembled here in 1189 before venturing forth to the Holy Land – a bloody endeavour that ultimately failed in its mission to capture Jerusalem from Saladin. Whether or not the Crusaders did meet here is a matter of debate, but the embellishment that their fellow Crusader King Richard I, aka Richard the Lionheart, joined them for a quaff is pretty much impossible to believe. Whatever the truth, the pub's pretty, whitewashed exterior, parts of which date back to the 17th century, is a singularly inviting prelude to the series of snug little bars that lie within.

Most of these bars are tunnelled into the sandstone of the rock that rises behind, with a short flight of interior stairs climbing up to the Rock Lounge, where a dusty, cobwebbed model galleon is protected within a glass case. It's dusty for a reason: the last three people who cleaned it are said to have died mysterious and unexpected deaths within a few months of doing so – hence its moniker as the 'cursed galleon'. It used to hang from the ceiling, but presumably it's now in a case to stop it from falling to pieces, rather than for fear of its magical properties. Galleon apart, the pub sports all manner of ancient decoration, but it's likely that these 'cave bars' were originally used as a brewhouse for the castle garrison.

The Trip, as locals call the place, assumed its present name in the 1790s, having previously been called The Pilgrim. It's now part of the multi-headed Greene King chain and offers nine cask ales daily. Filling pub food is also served, as well as a reasonable range of wines – and even, heaven forfend, cocktails.

Address 1 Brewhouse Yard, Nottingham, NG1 6AD, +44 (0)115 947 3171, www.greeneking-pubs.co.uk | **Getting there** Local bus (most lines) or tram to the city centre, then a five-minute walk | **Hours** Daily 11am–11pm | **Tip** Behind the railings to the rear of Ye Olde Trip is the Brewhouse Yard, where a brick-gabled block of 18th-century houses once accommodated some of the city's framework knitters. There are plans to turn the complex into a museum, but there is no definite opening date at time of writing.

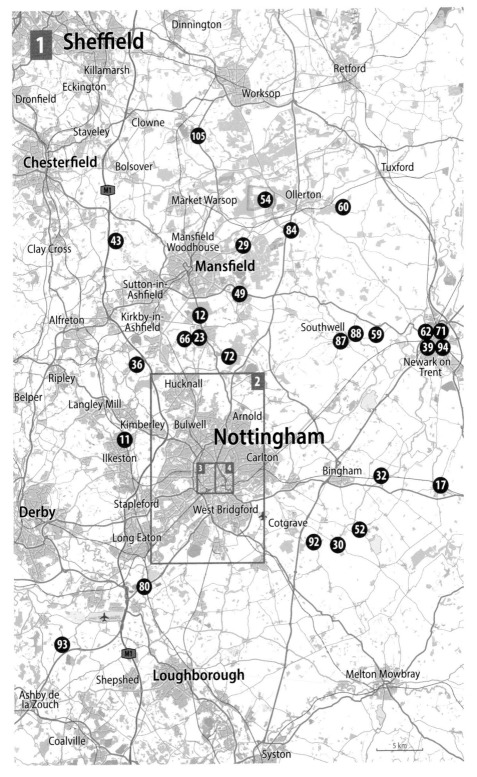

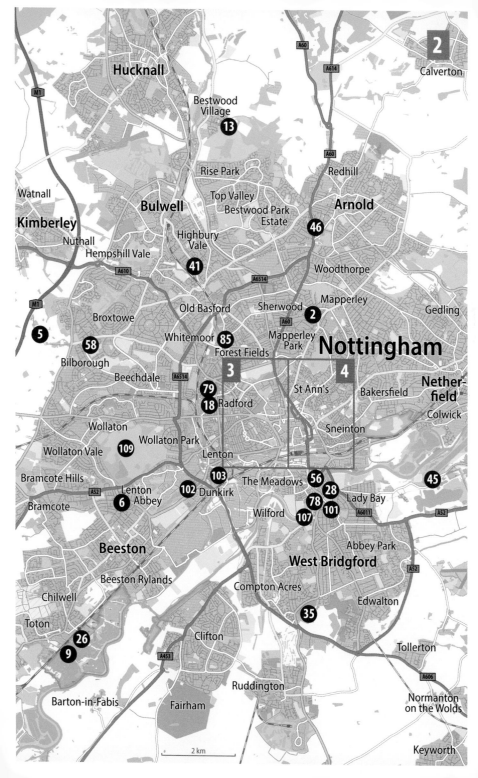

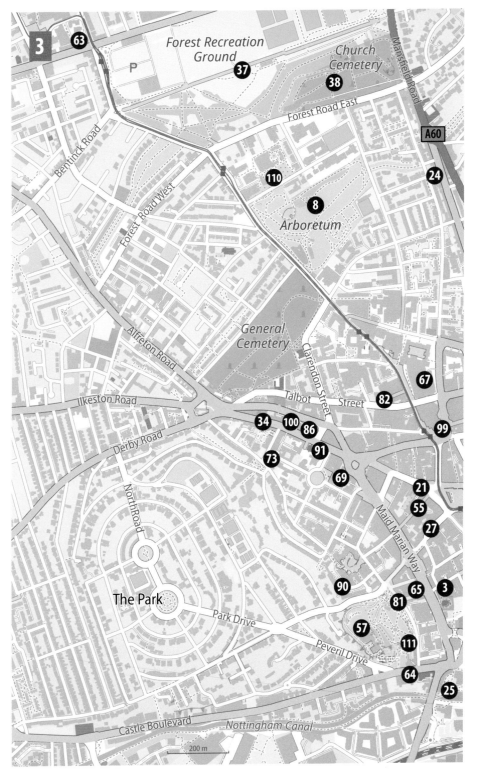

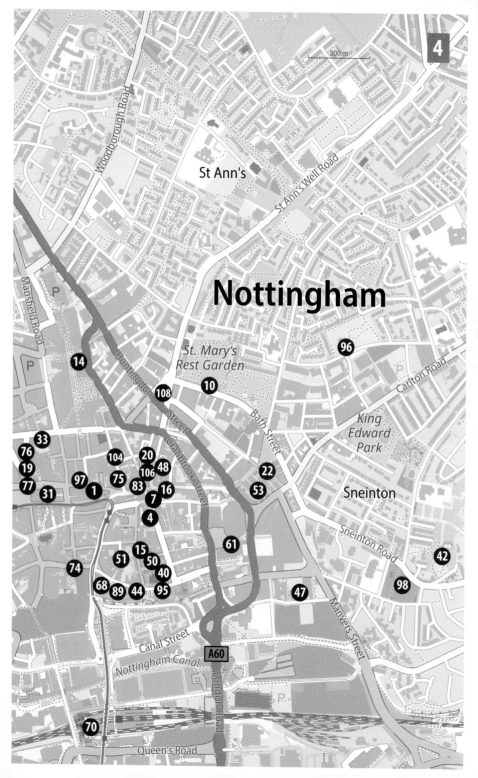

Ben Waddington
**111 Places in Birmingham
That You Shouldn't Miss**
ISBN 978-3-7408-2268-2

Michael Glover,
Richard Anderson
**111 Places in Sheffield
That You Shouldn't Miss**
ISBN 978-3-7408-2348-1

Julian Treuherz,
Peter de Figueiredo
**111 Places in Manchester
That You Shouldn't Miss**
ISBN 978-3-7408-2246-0

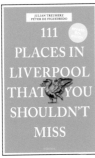

Julian Treuherz,
Peter de Figueiredo
**111 Places in Liverpool
That You Shouldn't Miss**
ISBN 978-3-7408-1607-0

Kim Revill, Alesh Compton
**111 Places in Leeds
That You Shouldn't Miss**
ISBN 978-3-7408-2059-6

David Taylor
**111 Places along Hadrian's Wall
That You Shouldn't Miss**
ISBN 978-3-7408-1425-0

David Taylor
**111 Places in Newcastle
That You Shouldn't Miss**
ISBN 978-3-7408-1043-6

Ed Glinert, David Taylor
**111 Places in Yorkshire
That You Shouldn't Miss**
ISBN 978-3-7408-1167-9

Lindsay Sutton, David Taylor
**111 Places in Lancaster
and Morecambe That You
Shouldn't Miss**
ISBN 978-3-7408-1557-8

Solange Berchemin
111 Places in the Lake District
That You Shouldn't Miss
ISBN 978-3-7408-1861-6

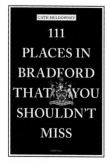

Cath Muldowney
111 Places in Bradford
That You Shouldn't Miss
ISBN 978-3-7408-1427-4

Katherine Bebo, Oliver Smith
111 Places in Poole
That You Shouldn't Miss
ISBN 978-3-7408-0598-2

Katherine Bebo, Oliver Smith
111 Places in Bournemouth
That You Shouldn't Miss
ISBN 978-3-7408- 1166-2

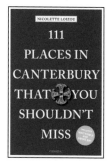

Nicolette Loizou
111 Places in Canterbury
That You Shouldn't Miss
ISBN 978-3-7408-0899-0

Rob Ganley, Ian Williams
111 Places in Coventry
That You Shouldn't Miss
ISBN 978-3-7408-1044-3

Martin Booth, Barbara Evripidou
111 Places in Bristol
That You Shouldn't Miss
ISBN 978-3-7408-2001-5

Alexandra Loske
111 Places in Brighton and
Lewes That You Shouldn't Miss
ISBN 978-3-7408-1727-5

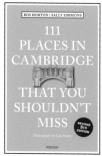

Rosalind Horton,
Sally Simmons, Guy Snape
111 Places in Cambridge
That You Shouldn't Miss
ISBN 978-3-7408-1285-0

Photo credits

Alabasters of Strelley (ch. 5): Phil Lee; Bennerley Viaduct (ch. 11): Mat Sirrell; Bessie Sheppard (ch. 12): Peter Smith; Bestwood Colliery (ch. 13): Phil Lee; Boulevard Works (ch. 18): Phil Lee; Byron at Newstead Abbey (ch. 23): Phil Lee; Colston Bassett (ch. 30): Peter Smith; Cranmer's Mound (ch. 32): Peter Smith; Edwin Starr's Grave (ch. 35): Phil Lee; Gannets (ch. 39): Peter Smith; Hardwick Hall (ch. 43): Peter Smith; Junction Fish Bar (ch. 49): Peter Smith; The Major Oak (ch. 54): Lucy Hodson (top), Colin Wilkinson (bottom); Mortimer's Hole (ch. 58): Tracey Whitefoot; Museum of Timekeeping (ch. 59): Phil Lee; National Holocaust Museum (ch. 60): Peter Smith; Newark Castle (ch. 62): Peter Smith; Newstead Abbey Gardens (ch. 66): Phil Lee; Ossington Coffee Palace (ch. 71): Peter Smith; Papplewick Pumping Station (ch. 72): David Bennett; Radford Boulevard Clock (ch. 79): Peter Smith; Southwell Workhouse (ch. 88): Peter Smith; St Mary Magdalene (ch. 94): Phil Lee; Welbeck Abbey (ch. 105): Peter Smith; Wollaton Hall (ch. 109): Phil Lee

Acknowledgements

So many friends and acquaintances have chipped in with ideas for this book, I hardly know where to begin. But I do want to thank Rod Wood and Cathy Rees; Martin Dunford for all his advice; Chez Abrams for knowing where to eat in north Nottinghamshire; Ruth Rigby, the musical tipster; Miriam Jackson of the Nottingham Women's History Group; David & Claire Fox; Rosemary Walker of All Saints, Strelley; John Scruton of the Friends of Bennerley Viaduct; Bradley Rice of Jamcafé; Simon Harrison of Danish Homestore; Adam Field; John Noble of Papplewick Pumping Station; Dave Robson for his tips on the origins of Broadway; Viv and Ron McCrossen for lots of tips and ideas; Brandon Harris of Smalleys; Luisa's Vegan Chocolates; Glenn Formoy of Southwell Minster; Kamala Newton of Nottingham High School; Jenny Rose; Rob James of Sherwood Forest NNR; David Young for his help with Nottingham castle; and Peter Smith for all his companionship and for assisting with the photographs. Last but not least, a big thank you to the photographer, Rachel Ghent, and Laura Olk of Emons, the publisher, for all her patience, hard work and attention to detail as she has guided me through the creation of this book.

Phil Lee

I would like to thank the following people: Simon Ghent for his continual support, encouragement and weekend bag carrying. Wilf, Lachlan, Savvi and Russ for helping out. DJ extraordinaire Stuart Hemulen. Bradley from Jam Cafe. The lovely staff at All Saints for being super helpful and allowing me to photograph the Stone Monkey in their store.

Rachel Ghent

Phil Lee was born and raised in Nottingham and he just couldn't escape the clutches of his home city, returning after a spell as a merchant seaman in the Danish navy. He lives there still, very happily, and has carved out a varied career as a travel writer.

Rachel Ghent was born in the North East England, where she studied photography at art college in Newcastle. After living in regions of the UK she has finally settled near Nottingham the first place she's ever felt at home and it's here you sipping natural wine in Jam Café or tucking into Sur The Angel Microbrewery.